The Baker Pocket Guide to
World Religions

D1166495

Other Books by Gerald R. McDermott

Claiming Christ: A Mormon-Evangelical Debate (with Robert Millet)

God's Rivals: Why God Allows Different Religions—Insights from the Bible and the Early Church

Jonathan Edwards Confronts the Gods: Christian Theology, Enlightenment Religion, and Non-Christian Faiths

Can Evangelicals Learn from Non-Christian Religions? Jesus, Revelation and the Religions

One Holy and Happy Society: The Public Theology of Jonathan Edwards

Understanding Jonathan Edwards: Introducing America's Theologian

Seeing God: Jonathan Edwards and Spiritual Discernment

Cancer: A Medical and Theological Guide for Patients and Their Families (with William A. Fintel, M.D.)

The Baker Pocket Guide to
World Religions

What Every Christian Needs to Know

Gerald R. McDermott

BakerBooks

a division of Baker Publishing Group
Grand Rapids, Michigan

This book is dedicated to my excellent friend and coauthor,
one of the best oncologists in the world, Bill Fintel.
He has helped me think about and write this
and many other books.

Published by Baker Books
a division of Baker Publishing Group
P.O. Box 6287, Grand Rapids, MI 49516-6287
www.bakerbooks.com

Printed in the United States of America

Library of Congress Cataloging-in-Publication Data
McDermott, Gerald R. (Gerald Robert)
    The Baker pocket guide to world religions : what every Christian needs to
know / Gerald R. McDermott.
        p.   cm.
    Includes bibliographical references.
    ISBN 978-0-8010-7160-7 (pbk.)
    1. Religions. I. Title. II. Title: Pocket guide to world religions.
BL80.3.M33 2008
200—dc22

2008002963

Contents

Acknowledgments

I am deeply grateful to the following friends and colleagues for reading parts of the manuscript and giving expert advice: Alan Pieratt, Robert Benne, Mark Graham, Bill Fintel, Shang Quanyu, Brian Mahoney, Reginald Shareef, Karl Uotinen, Marwood Larson-Harris, and our good friends at the Northampton Seminar. My students in the fall 2007 iteration of Christian Theology and World Religions made helpful suggestions. I am appreciative of the adult VBS class at St. John Lutheran Church in Roanoke, whose members listened so well and helped me know what would and would not work for a broad audience. Byron Johnson and the Baylor Institute for Studies of Religion gave me the critical support I needed to carve out part of a summer for writing. Karen Harris helped me with some technical problems, as she has for other books, and she also gave a great suggestion. Thanks are also due to my student assistant Ella Wade for her help in preparing the final manuscript. Most importantly, my wife, Jean, as always, managed house and home and helped me think through things, so that I could write.

When Did the Religions Start?
A Timeline

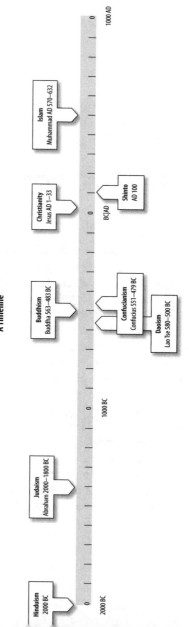

Hinduism
2000 BC

Judaism
Abraham 2000–1800 BC

Buddhism
Buddha 563–483 BC

Confucianism
Confucius 551–479 BC

Daoism
Lao Tse 580–500 BC

Christianity
Jesus AD 1–33

Shinto
AD 100

Islam
Muhammad AD 570–632

2000 BC

1000 BC

BC|AD

0

1000 AD

Why Study the World Religions?

Or, Ignorance Is Not Bliss

Let me guess—you're a Christian who is very busy. You know from the news, and your own neighbors, that the world religions are becoming more important every day. You also know that Christians are to share the good news of Jesus and that in today's pluralistic society this often means talking to folks who already have a religion, usually one of the major religions of the world. Not only that, but you're just plain interested in what others believe. The deeper you grow in your own faith, the more curious you have become about the faith of others. Just what do they believe? And why do they do what they do? But you don't have time to read a big academic book on the world religions. You're afraid you might not understand it anyway.

This book is for you. It is short and concise and will give you an easy-to-understand overview of the most important beliefs (and some practices) of those who belong to the six most important non-Christian religions in the world—Hinduism, Judaism, Buddhism, the Confucianism-Daoism combination of Chinese religion, Shinto, and Islam. It even has a chapter on your own faith, Christianity, so that you can understand and explain it better. Each chapter is self-contained, so if you don't have time right now to read the first few chapters but want to go right to Islam, for example, you can do so without losing anything important.

But first, let's get the lay of the land—the globe, that is. How many believers in the various religions are there? Here are some 2007 stats[1] from two top experts on global religious statistics, David B. Barrett and Todd M. Johnson:

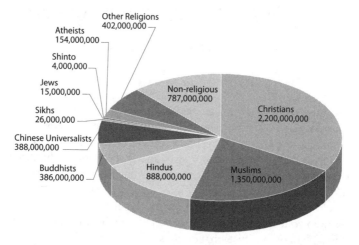

There are many more world religions, but these are the most recognizable and some of the most important. Notice these interesting facts:

1. Christians number exactly one-third of the world population.
2. Muslims are more than one-fifth.

3. That means that one-half of the world is either Muslim or Christian.

Another fact of interest is the relatively small combined number of atheists and nonreligious (the nonreligious are the folks who say, "I am spiritual but don't believe in organized religion")—941 million, or only 14 percent of the world's population. Atheists are 2 percent. That percentage seems to decline as the years progress. This means that what many of us heard from our college professors—that secularism is on the increase—was wrong. Peter Berger, distinguished sociologist at Boston University and one of the proponents of that secularization thesis, recently conceded, "We were wrong."[2] In other words, secularism is not on the rise—religion is. Faith is gaining on nearly every continent (not Christian faith necessarily, but faith in one of the major religions), and that seems likely to be the case for decades to come.

The Value of Learning about Other Religions

Perhaps you're a bit wary of learning about other religions. (If not, you can skip this section.) You may have been told that learning about other faiths can diminish your own. Or perhaps you think that with your limited time, you should concentrate only on Scripture and Christian theology. There's actually something to be said for spending a large chunk of your available study time on these. But consider the following reasons for learning at least some characteristics of other religions. You will gain understanding of your world, become more effective in your witness, understand your own faith better, become a better disciple, and work better with others.

Learn about Your World

The recent terrorist attacks and wars in the Middle East and Afghanistan have shown that we cannot understand our world without understanding its religions. Think especially of the war in Iraq, which after 2005 turned into a civil war between Sunnis and Shi'ites. How can we understand that unless we understand how those two Muslim sects differ?

In 1978 President Jimmy Carter asked the CIA for a report on an American ally, the Shah of Iran. The CIA reassured the President that all was well and the Peacock Throne was stable. Just months later the Shah was driven from his throne by the Iranian Revolution, and the world has not been the same since. How could the CIA have been so wrong? They thought they could understand the politics of Iran without studying its religion.

The same thing can be said for nearly every other part of the world—Israel/Palestine (with its obvious Jewish, Muslim, and Christian underpinnings), India and its nationalist parties (rooted in Hindu convictions), and East Asia's economic strength (ineradicably connected with its Confucianist legacy), to give just a few examples. To understand a people, we must have some understanding of their religion.

There's a simple reason for all of this. The vast majority of the world's people are religious, and at the very deepest level of their being, it is their religion that governs them. We can't even begin to understand them without knowing something of their religions.

Effective Witness

We Christians know that Jesus commanded us to make disciples of all nations (Matt. 28:18–20). We also know that he commanded us to love our neighbors as ourselves (Mark 12:33) and to follow the Golden Rule (Matt. 7:12), treating others the way we want to be treated.

I appreciate people who treat me with sensitivity and respect, and I should treat others with sensitivity and respect, especially those with whom I am trying to share the gospel. So that means I should try to understand my non-Christian neighbor's religion before I tell him about my own. Suppose my neighbor already believes in a god of grace (as many Hindus and Buddhists do), and I assume he knows only a god of law, and our conversation reveals my lack of understanding to him. In other words, he believes his god forgives sins out of sheer love, but I assume his god will only punish sins and not forgive them. Not only will I fail to show him the courtesy of my understanding, but I will fail miserably in my role as an evangelist. If I study his religion, I may find that what he really wants to hear is not about grace but history—whether God ever really entered history. That will make my witness more effective.

Understanding Your Faith

Many Christians have reported that they understood their own faith better after learning about other faiths. Jesus' grace is more real after studying the works-oriented schemes (based on the idea that we are saved only if we are good enough) in some religions. Jesus' real life in real history seems more significant after learning that the stories of the most popular Hindu savior (Krishna) are mythological. And Christian moral teachings are more credible when we discover that all the major religions agree on basic moral principles.

Be a Better Disciple

I remember growing closer to Jesus Christ by reading Watchman Nee's description of the believer's union with Christ, in his book *The Normal Christian Life*. Nee seemed to have a deeper understanding of that union than any Westerner I had read. Years later

I discovered that Nee's depth was partly a result of growing up in China, where Daoism had saturated the culture with a vision of personal oneness with the divine. Of course Daoist union is quite different from Christian union, but Nee's cultural background was closer to the cultural background of the Bible on this question of how the individual is related to other persons and God. It helped him see some New Testament realities more clearly than most of us who are raised in a culture steeped in individualism. Studying other religions can give us such insights and help us better understand the Bible, and thereby more closely follow our Lord.

Christians have also been moved to a deeper commitment to Christ when seeing other believers' devotion to their lords and causes. For example, the Dalai Lama's refusal to hate the Chinese despite Chinese massacres of hundreds of thousands of Tibetan Buddhists has deepened the resolve of some Christians to imitate Jesus' example of loving his enemies.

Working with Others

When we have some understanding of the beliefs of others, we can work more effectively with them toward common social and moral goals. At the 1995 United Nations Conference on Population and Development in Cairo, an American delegation was working furiously to enshrine abortion on demand as a universal human right. They were defeated only after Roman Catholics, directed by the Vatican, joined forces with mainstream Muslims. Catholics and Muslims disagree on who God is and how to reach him, but they agree that abortion is wrong and not a "right" on par with other human rights. If you study the religions, you will find that, while Christian theology is quite different from that of other religions, its moral teachings are similar to that of others. Christians may want to work with believers from other traditions in the future to fight poverty, racism, infanticide, euthanasia, human cloning, and stem cell research that creates and destroys human embryos. But they will be able to do so only if they have some understanding of what these other believers believe.

An Overview

Are you convinced you should learn about the religions? If so, let's start with the oldest (see the timeline on p. 8) set of world religions, the disparate collection of beliefs and practices collectively known as Hinduism. Then we will move, in chronological order, to Judaism, Buddhism, Confucianism and Daoism, Christianity, Shinto and Japanese New Religions, and finally Islam. We'll conclude by answering two very common questions: Can or should we evangelize people who already have a religion? Can we learn from other religions?

One last thing. This is not a *comprehensive* book with something about *everything* religious. It isn't a dictionary or encyclopedia of the world religions. Nor does it cover every last religion in the world—or every subset of the major religions. It doesn't give you a huge list of details in every chapter. But it *does* give you a basic overview of the most important and visible religions, the ones you are most likely to encounter in your neighborhood or at the office or as you travel around the world. Rather than giving you a mind-numbing collection of facts, it will help you understand how people in these religions *think*. In every chapter there is at least one personal testimony written by a believer in that religion. The book also provides a thumbnail sketch of some of the most important issues related to these religions. For example, the Islam chapter has sidebars on Islam and women and on Islam and democracy, while the chapter on Hinduism has sidebars on Gandhi, the caste system in India, and the most popular gods. Note that there is a glossary that defines unfamiliar terms and identifies people mentioned in the text.

Finally, this book will give you a concise Christian perspective on each of these major world religions—to help you figure out how your faith compares and how you should relate to people whose beliefs are different from yours. These are very important for a Christian to know. You will then be able to understand better not only other religions but your own as well.

The Four Questions

In every chapter you will see a table that will answer four questions. The answers to these questions will provide you with a thumbnail sketch of each religion or kind of religion.

1. What is the *ultimate concern*? (This means the final goal adherents are seeking.)
2. What is this religion's *view of reality*?
   a. God or the gods (Are they real? What are they like? Can they help us?)
   b. The human self (What is human nature? For example, is it bad, good, created, divine?)
   c. The physical world (Is it real, eternal or created, bad or good?)
3. What is the basic human problem?
4. How is the basic human problem resolved?

Hinduisms

The World's Oldest Set of Religions

There is no such thing as Hinduism. (You now know more than the average Christian and will immediately stand out in your next theological debate.) The term *Hinduism* implies a religion in which the parts are consistent with one another. But such a religion does not exist. That will no doubt surprise you, but consider this: the word *Hinduism* is a word the British coined as a catchall term for the innumerable and often contradictory religions they found on the Indian subcontinent.

I say contradictory because, for example, some Indian religions are theistic (they believe in a personal god) and others aren't. The latter think the divine is an it, not a Someone. This *it* includes everything and contains everything (this is called pantheism), but it most certainly is not a Person who created the world or to whom we can pray.

That's the reason I say some Indian religions contradict others. Theistic Indian religions contradict pantheistic Indian religions. And these pantheistic religions can actually be called atheistic because their adherents don't believe in a personal god who created the world or who can save us. They are religious (they have a reverence for the mystery and spiritual essence of the world) but atheistic (there is no personal god who created or rules the world).

Now, most Hindus probably would not agree that these different religions are contradictory. They would say either that it doesn't matter because religious practice is most important, or that what seems contradictory to us is really harmonious at the "highest" level of reality. (I will explain "levels of reality" in just a bit.) Some of these Hindus talk about Hinduism as a journey in which they progress from worshiping a god to realizing that the god is merely an image of ultimate reality in which there are no personal gods.

But back to my first point. Instead of one religion called Hinduism, there are many religions in India, often contradictory and wildly conflicting in beliefs. That's the reason I have titled this chapter "Hinduisms: The World's Oldest Set of Religions." A more accurate title would be "the native religions of India." I say "native" because Christianity, Islam, and Buddhism (as well as others) are also flourishing religions in India, with millions of adherents there, but they were founded elsewhere.[1] This chapter will focus on Indian religions that got their start on the Indian subcontinent.

There are many, many different religions that are called Hindu. The Hindu scriptures in fact say there are 330 million gods and at least several scores of these gods have their own sets of beliefs and practices. So where to start?

I think the best way to make some sense of this huge number of competing and mutually conflicting Indian religions is to look at two things about life and death that almost all Hindus believe in, and then to see the two major sets of Indian religions (all called Hindu) that try to resolve those two things.

In Agreement on Two Concepts

The first thing most Hindus agree on is *samsara*. This is pretty much what we call reincarnation. Hindus call it the combination of *karma* (literally, "deeds") and rebirth. It means that after death we are judged by an impersonal law of karma, which determines what kind of life we will be reborn into. If we did bad deeds and therefore have bad karma, we are reborn into an unhappy life as a human being or animal or even insect. If we led a good life and accumulated good karma, then we will be reborn into a happy human life. Samsara is the endless (and without beginning, either) cycle of life, death, and rebirth: after each life we die and are reborn into a different life.

Shirley MacLaine may look forward to her coming rebirths, but in the history of India, most Hindus haven't. Life has usually not been too happy for most Hindus, and most of them know they may not have what it takes to earn a better rebirth the next time around. Therefore most Hindus earnestly seek the second thing most of them agree on: *moksha*.

Moksha is Sanskrit for "liberation," which in this case means liberation or release from the iron law of samsara. In other words, Hindus want to be released from the iron law of life-death-rebirth. They don't *want* to be reborn forever and ever. They want to stop the wheel and get off—finally to be free of reincarnation. Most of

Advaita devotees say yoga is the process by which one comes to knowledge of Brahman (the impersonal essence and spirit of the cosmos). Other Hindus use the word *yoga*, however, to refer to any systematic program of meditation. Most think of yoga as an eight-stage program developed by Patanjali that starts with body posture and breathing as means to focus on the essence of the universe. Then one is to retract the senses and withdraw into a realm where individual selfhood seems illusory, and one realizes the final reality where there are no distinctions.

the assorted varieties of Hindu religions can be seen as ways to get free from samsara and therefore to achieve *moksha*.

Four Roads to *Moksha*

There are four main avenues in Hindu religions to *moksha*: the way of knowledge (*jnana*, the best-known of which is Advaita Vedanta), the way of devotion (*bhakti*), the way of works (*karma*), and the way of meditation (*yoga*). We are going to look at two of these, because they are the best known and the most widely practiced—the way of knowledge and the way of devotion. The first, the way of knowledge or Advaita Vedanta, is the best known and most prestigious intellectual tradition in Hinduism, and the second, the way of devotion (bhakti), is far and away the most popular form of Hindu religion today. If you can get a basic idea of how these two Hindu systems work, you will be able to comprehend the basic ways the vast majority of Hindus in the world think.

The Way of Knowledge: Advaita Vedanta

Take off your Western eyeglasses and be ready to imagine a way of looking at reality that is very different from your own. With a little patience, you can conceive a world as it is seen by more than a billion people on this planet (because some features of this philosophy are shared by Daoists and Buddhists).

This way to *moksha* is called the way of knowledge because it promises that you can escape samsara (the endless cycle of life-death-rebirth) if you come to see (know) reality in the right way. It takes a lot of work to come to this knowledge or spiritual vision, but the result will be the end to rebirths (reincarnation).

The most famous teacher of this way was Shankara (AD 788–820), a Brahmin (see the sidebar) priest and philosopher from south India. Shankara's system, which has become the most respected school of philosophy for Hindus, is called Advaita Vedanta.

Understanding what *Advaita* and *Vedanta* mean will help us understand this all-important philosophy. *Advaita* is Sanskrit for "non-dual." This means there are not two (or three or more) things in reality. In other words, there is ultimately only one thing. That one thing is Brahman, the impersonal spirit or essence of the cosmos, and it is unchanging. Everything that appears to our eyes and other senses is ultimately unreal. Only eyes that have been opened spiritually can see the underlying reality in all things.

Vedanta means "end of the Vedas." The Vedas are the early set of Hindu scriptures, the last set of which (the "end" of them) are the Upanishads. These writings, composed between 600 and 400 BC, teach that the human self (atman) is the same as the essence of the cosmos (Brahman).

Shankara taught that typically we think anything that is real is distinct from other real things and is always changing. So, for example, I think that I am separate from the computer at which I am now looking, and that both the computer and I are constantly changing. But if I were to attain spiritual knowledge, I would "see" that both the computer and I share an unchanging inner reality, and that this inner essence is more real than the outer

There are thousands of levels in the caste system, but the most basic categories are these:

1. Brahmins or priests: today these include genealogists, astrologers, and physicians practicing traditional medicine.
2. Kshatriyas: rulers and leaders traditionally, but today landowners engaged in farming.
3. Vaisyas: those who keep official records and shopkeepers, moneylenders, goldsmiths, dealers in grain and vegetable oils.
4. Shudras: menial artisans, laborers, and servants, including carpenters, blacksmiths, barbers, potters, and tailors.
5. Untouchables: technically not a caste at all; other castes think they will be polluted by bodily contact with untouchables.

The Indian constitution forbids discrimination on the basis of caste, but most Hindus believe birth into a caste has been determined by the impersonal law of karma and rebirth.

forms people see when they look at me and my computer as two different things.

Notice I said "more real." Usually we in the West think in terms of reality and unreality. I am real and the character in a movie—say, Spiderman—is unreal. But in India people think in terms of *levels* of reality. They would point to a nightmare, in which a bogeyman is chasing us—a dream I confess I have from time to time. When I am dreaming this, my heart beats faster and I may even sweat because I am afraid. Is the bogeyman real? To my dreaming mind, he is very real! That's why I sweat and my heart beats faster. But to my conscious mind, just after I awake and realize in relief it was only a dream, the bogeyman is unreal. Hindus would say that, at least while I was dreaming, that bogeyman was real—but at a lower level of reality.

We Christians might say that Jesus Christ is *more* real than I am. He was and is the *fully* real human being, fully actualized. Christians connected to him are also real, but because of our sins and incomplete sanctification, our humanity is far less real than his. In other words, when we look at Jesus, we see full humanity. When someone looks at me, she does not see a full man because I am not what God fully intended a human being to be. I am not as really human as Jesus was and is. Humans are meant to love always and love deeply, and my love is sporadic and often superficial. So in this sense we too might say that I am less real, or on a lower level of reality, than Jesus.

This Christian way of talking about levels of reality is different from the Hindu one, but it may help you imagine how Hindus can talk this way. For example, Shankara taught that the gods, human beings, and the world are all real, but at a lower level of reality from that which is at the highest level—Brahman. Each member of these three groups (gods, human beings, and physical world[s]) exists, but only as that bogeyman in my dream exists. Or as a murder in a stage play exists. In the drama on the stage, there really are people fighting one another, a murder weapon, (at least fake) blood, and cries of pain. And the people in the audience really do feel excitement and shock and sadness—but only at the level of the play. They know that at a "higher" level (as Hindus would say) or in "real life" (as Westerners would say), there was no murder.

So too for the gods. They have a "certain" reality in our lives here and now. But when all is said and done and we see reality as it really is, we will realize that they are not part of what is fully real.

Neither is this world fully real. It is like when we are walking in the forest at dusk and look ahead on the trail and see what looks very much like a snake. We get scared (if you're like me—I hate snakes!) and stop walking forward, wondering how in the world we can get to our destination by another route. When we realize there is no other way, and we inch forward to get a better

Vishnu is the greatest of the bhakti gods. He is believed to have come to earth nine times to set things right, each time in the form of an animal or man. These incarnations, called *avataras*, were as a fish, tortoise, boar, man-lion, dwarf, high-caste hero, Rama, Krishna, and Buddha.

The two most important *avatars* (incarnate forms) of Vishnu were as Rama and Krishna. *Krishna* is the hero of the *Bhagavad-Gita*, the most popular Hindu scripture.

The Hare Krishnas worship Krishna exclusively as the lord of the cosmos.

There is a Hindu trinity of sorts: *Brahma* (to be distinguished from the impersonal Brahman and the caste of Brahmin priests) as creator, Vishnu as preserver, and Shiva as destroyer. *Lakshmi*, Vishnu's consort, is the goddess of wealth.

Shiva is also called the god of the totality that includes both creation and destruction, and is beyond the distinction between matter and spirit. His wife or consort is *Shakti*, who represents the tangible world with all of its dangers. She has been worshiped in various forms, including as *Kali*, who is pictured with four arms, a necklace of skulls, and waistband of severed arms. Her tongue hangs out to lap up blood. Shiva is worshiped inside temples that usually have an upright stone phallus, called the *lingam*.

Hanuman is the monkey-king in the *Ramayana*, a great Hindu epic. He is also a god of strength, loyalty, and learning and is a symbol of the servant in relation to his master.

Ganesha is the elephant-faced son of Shiva, worshiped as the overcomer of obstacles at the beginning of rites and undertakings.

The goddess *Durga* is worshiped especially in west Bengal, as the Divine Warrior, often riding on a tiger or lion. She conquers evil and brings peace.

look, we are suddenly relieved to discover it is only a rope. We conclude that the snake was only an illusion ("maya" in Sanskrit). Shankara said the separate human individual and even the world itself are also maya. The only thing that is "really" real is Brahman, where there are no distinctions between any one thing and anything else.

Hard to understand? Some Hindus have used the illustration of a drop of water falling out of the sky over the ocean. While that drop is falling, it is an individual drop, with unique characteristics, like no other drop in the world. It has a unique weight, density, shape, taste, color, and even smell—though the way in which each of these is different from those of other drops is infinitesimally small. Nevertheless, it is a drop like no other in the world. So it is a distinct, individual drop.

Yet when that drop hits the surface of the ocean, in less than a second it loses its individuality. No longer does it have a shape or weight or density. Now the atoms of that drop are dispersed throughout the ocean. Does the drop still exist? Yes and no. No, as a drop with individuality. But yes, insofar as the particles and molecules of that drop are still around, but they have become merged with the ocean itself. There is now no distinction between the drop and the ocean.

Hindus who adhere to this Advaita tradition compare us in our individual selves to that drop, and our future in Brahman to the ocean a moment after that drop has hit the surface. In Brahman there is no "I." But in some way that you and I (and even Shankara!) cannot understand, "we" still have some degree of existence, yet not as individual selves.

Let's sum up by asking how Shankara thinks we can solve the basic human problem. You see, every religion says this world is not the way it is supposed to be, that the cosmos has been screwed up in some way. This is what I mean by "the basic human problem."

Every religion also prescribes what it thinks is the resolution to the basic human problem. I will explain for Shankara, and for bhakti in the next few pages, their answers to both of these questions: What is the basic human problem? And how can it be resolved?

Shankara said that the basic human problem is ignorance. By the way, most religions of the Far East say the same, though each defines the object of the ignorance—what we are ignorant *of*—differently. While most Hindu and Buddhist religions say the human problem is intellectual, Christianity, Islam, and Judaism, the religions that began in the Middle East, say the basic human problem is moral. Let me repeat that for clarity's sake: in the Far East the basic problem

---

Gandhi

Gandhi (1869–1948), a great Indian leader, was trained as a lawyer in England. Known as Mahatma (great-souled), he led India's fight for independence from Britain. Gandhi took elements from Jesus' teachings and the *Bhagavad-Gita* to teach *ahimsa*, "noninjury" in Sanskrit.

Gandhi said violence is a method for the weak, and nonviolence requires more courage. In his battle against the British, he taught his followers to hate British acts but not the British. They were to believe that even if they died in the struggle, truth would prevail. Ahimsa, he said, is the truth behind all religions.

Gandhi's teachings have given greater prominence to nonviolence in Hindu religions.

Hindu Priests

Hindu priests have different functions. Some maintain a temple; others specialize in weddings; others are genealogists or astrologers or physicians of traditional medicine. They are generally paid by the temple or freewill offering.

is said to be intellectual, while the religions of the Middle East tell us our basic problem is moral.

According to Shankara, of what are we ignorant? The answer is Brahman, or ultimate reality, which of course contains no distinctions and therefore is finally only one thing.

How do we solve the problem? By meditation and asceticism (that's coming up). That means we must meditate on the nature of reality until we finally "see" that everything is Brahman, even the individual self (atman). But we will attain that final vision only if we combine asceticism with meditation. This is when we deprive ourselves of the pleasures of the flesh, such as tasty food and drink, a soft bed, sex and marriage, and other sensual enjoyments. Hindus seeking Brahman will often go into the forest to meditate, where they will sleep on the ground and eat the barest of foods, often fasting.

The Way of Devotion: Bhakti

Now that we have explored the most prestigious Hindu path to moksha, let's turn to the most *popular* path. It is called *bhakti*, which is Sanskrit for "devotion." This path is a way to liberation from samsara (remember, this is the endless cycle of reincarnation) by means of love and surrender (devotion) to a personal god.

Notice I use the adjective "personal." This is because the previous path, Advaita, says that the gods are not real at the highest level of reality. So there is no personal god at all. Brahman is not a person (having mind, will, and emotions) and not a god as we tend to think—a Someone who created the world and controls it and will finally put an end to it. No, Brahman is impersonal, something of an *it* that is behind and in the world, and in fact is the only thing that is unchanging and fully real.

But *bhaktas* (devotees of bhakti) believe there are gods, and they are at every level of reality, if there are levels at all. (Some

think there is truth in Advaita Vedanta, others don't.) Some of the gods are very powerful and can actually save us from samsara. They do this by forgiving our sins and getting rid of our bad karma, so that we can live with them forever in one of their heavens. And rather than going through many lives, trying to build up good karma and getting rid of bad karma, they will do this for us after *this* life if we turn to them in sincere faith. It is no wonder that bhakti is far more popular than Advaita or any other way. It is easier (by far!) and much faster.

Take Krishna, for example, who is the most popular of all the Hindu gods, and the main character and speaker in the most beloved Hindu scripture, the *Bhagavad-Gita*. Krishna is said to be an incarnation (avatar) of Vishnu, who came to earth to right wrongs and restore righteousness. If one of his devotees serves him with love and praise, he will be released from samsara and not be reborn but enter one of Krishna's lovely heavens.

As you can see from the previous paragraph, Hindu bhakti contains the idea of incarnation (a god coming to earth, literally "in the flesh"). Its chief god (different from its most popular god, who is Krishna) is Vishnu, the god of order and righteousness, who comes down from the heavens whenever evil is especially bad on earth, so that he can set things aright. Bhaktas believe Vishnu has come to earth in various incarnations nine times, and will come again at the end of time in a tenth incarnation (avatara). His previous incarnations have been as a fish, tortoise, boar, man-lion, dwarf, high-caste hero, Rama (another god), Krishna, and Buddha.

We've already seen that while those following Advaita do not believe in the final reality of personal gods and are therefore essentially atheistic, *bhaktas* are theists. Another difference is that *bhaktas* believe the human self is real and will retain its individuality even after release from samsara. There's no dissolution of the drop of water into the ocean for *bhaktas,* but they believe that the human self is divine, in fact, a "finite mode" of God.

Still other points of difference: *bhaktas* say the world is real and change is real, without different levels of reality. But this world is not a place of hope or fulfillment. As we have seen, most Hindus are pessimistic about their ability to have deep or lasting happiness here on earth.

For bhakti, the basic human problem is being stuck in samsara. What keeps us stuck is the combination of our karma and our ignorance of a personal god. The resolution to the problem is to get rid of karma by practicing love and surrender to a personal god (bhakti) and getting grace (prasada) from that god.

Many Christians have thought that their faith is the only one that teaches salvation by grace. Now you can see this is not the case (though bhakti may have developed after Hindus came into contact with Christianity).

It's interesting that there are two kinds of bhakti, and one teaches grace more radically than the other. The first is the monkey school (think of the baby monkey clinging to its mother) that says the god will give us grace only if we cooperate by purifying ourselves. You could say that the monkey school teaches salvation by grace and works.

> ### The Sacred Cow
>
> Many visitors to India are amazed by the reverence people have for cows and their refusal to slaughter them, when so many people are hungry. But the cow has been sacred from very early Hindu history. In early Hindu writings, the gods were said to be "cow-born" and the cosmic waters called "cows." The cow was a symbol of heaven, earth, and speech. The Indian epic *Mahabharata* says the killer of a cow will be reborn in hell for as many years as there are hairs on his body. Cows are associated with the Mother Goddess, who gave the cow to humanity for its five products—milk, butter, curds, dung, and urine. The cow is especially sacred to Shiva, was a part of the story of Krishna (he was a cowherd), and is a symbol of India as mother who provides for needs. Gandhi said the cow represents the indissoluble bond between humans and subhumans—an example of complete giving to others.

The cat school (think of the kitten doing nothing while being carried by its mother's teeth) says that salvation by Krishna, let's say (remember, there are other bhakti gods such as Rama), is entirely by Krishna's grace. Whatever we do to serve and love Krishna is only by his grace too.

Most bhaktas, however, believe human effort and merit are necessary. Krishna and the other gods wait to see who makes good efforts before they confer salvation.

Christian Analysis

What can we say as Christians about these Hindu religions? The first thing we can say is that there are obvious similarities. *Avataras* are similar to the Christian incarnation of Jesus Christ. Both Hindus and Christians say that God has come to earth to help and save.

There is also the idea of grace, which technically means God does for human beings what they cannot do for themselves.

But there are profound differences between Christianity and Hinduism. The *avataras*, as even Hindu scholars concede, are based less on historical reality than theological story. The stories about Krishna (stealing butter and having amorous affairs with cowgirls), for example, seem to have been a conflation of accounts of several Krishnas in real history, with supernatural elements added later. Second, there are ten incarnations in Hinduism, unlike the one incarnation of Jesus, which did all that was needed to save human beings for all time. Third, these Hindu saviors are less than morally perfect, while Jesus was sinless.

Christian grace is also different from bhakti grace. In the latter, grace is in the context of an impersonal law of the universe (karma), which even the gods cannot change. In Christian faith, on the other hand, Jesus Christ is the author of the law, and he has canceled the power of that law over us.

But more important, a self-indulgent Krishna forgives sins at no cost to himself. Jesus Christ, on the other hand, was sinless and gives us grace only by an infinitely painful atonement. Grace cost him everything.

There are other differences as well, between both Hindu schools and Christian faith:

1. *Ultimate concern*: For the Hindu, it is escape from the human condition; for the Christian it is freedom from guilt, sin, and the devil.
2. *Human nature*: For the Christian it is creaturely and sinful; for the Hindu it is divine.
3. *Human problem*: It is moral sin for the Christian and intellectual ignorance for the Hindu.
4. *Resolution*: For the Christian it is a divine act at infinite cost to God; for the Hindu it is human effort, sometimes mixed with grace, without cost to the god.

Judaism

*Christianity's Mother
and Older Brother*

Most Christians in the United States have
grown up with Jewish neighbors, classmates,
and friends, but their understanding of Judaism is usually limited to their reading of the
Old Testament and the holiday in December
called Chanukah. Some of us learned in Sunday
school that Judaism teaches salvation by works.
Many wonder how on earth Jews cannot see
that Jesus of Nazareth is the Messiah. In this
little chapter we will see that, typically, religious
Jews don't think in terms of being saved; that
even when they do, they don't believe they got
into the covenant because they deserved it; and
that they think they have biblical reasons for
rejecting Jesus as Messiah.

But first, let's get an overview of numbers and groups. How many Jews are there? And into what groups are they divided?

Numbers and Groups

In 2007 there were 15 million Jews worldwide, with 5 million in Israel and 6.5 million in the United States. Of the latter, 1.6 million are in New York State, and the vast majority of those are in New York City.

So you can see what a tiny religious group (compared to the other religions in this book) this is—6/10 of 1 percent of the number of Christians (2.2 billion) and 1 percent of the number of Muslims (1.36 billion). But this has always been the case, even before the Holocaust. The number of Jews in the world has always been tiny in comparison to their overwhelming significance as a religious people. I say "overwhelming" because their religion not only "invented" monotheism—at least after the prehistoric rise of polytheism—but it became the mother of both Christianity and Islam, the largest religions in the world. Often Pope John Paul II referred to Jews as "our older brothers" because they had come to know the true God before Christians saw him in Jesus Christ.[1]

In the United States, as in Israel and other countries, Jews are divided into two groups—religious Jews and secular Jews. The former believe in God and perpetuate the Jewish tradition in a variety of ways. The latter have either rejected the idea of God entirely or, while still believing in God, do not believe the Jewish tradition is the best or only way to God. Yet they take pride in the accomplishments of the Jewish people, including their spiritual creativity.

Religious Jews in the United States are generally divided into three movements: Reform, Conservative, and Orthodox. These are three different responses to the Enlightenment—the eighteenth-century intellectual movement that tended to reject religious tradition and embrace secular reason as the guide to all of life, both religious and secular.

The differences started in nineteenth-century Germany. Reform Jews accommodated themselves to Enlightenment culture, reducing their religion to what they thought simple and reasonable—ethical monotheism (there is one God and we should live moral lives). They used organs (a modern instrument then), prayed, and preached in German (not Hebrew), discarded prayer shawls and head coverings, let men and women sit together (this was new), and eliminated some kosher dietary rules (see sidebar). They also rejected Zionism, the movement to establish a homeland for Jews (see sidebar).

The Orthodox reacted against Reform, thinking the latter had sold out to modern culture. They prayed for the ultimate restoration of Zion (ancient biblical Israel), regarded the whole Old Testament as God's Word (the

Kosher Food

This term *kosher* comes from *kashrut* or "correct" (food). It refers to a set of dietary restrictions that forbid such things as animals that don't chew the cud and do not have a cloven hoof, carnivorous birds, winged insects, shellfish (without scales and fins), small creeping animals, and any animals that died by themselves or were slaughtered improperly. Meat and milk are not to be mixed. Many theories have been advanced to explain the reasoning for these rules, such as a concern for cleanliness and health, but generally their observance is thought to train believers in holiness.

Zionism

Zionism is a nineteenth-century movement led by Austro-Hungarian journalist Theodor Herzl (1860–1904) to seek a homeland for Jews because of their persecution since medieval times. Its culmination was the establishment of the state of Israel by the United Nations in 1948.

Kabbalah

Kabbalah means "reception" or "oral tradition." It is a movement that started in the thirteenth century AD, teaching special mystical traditions that are said to be understood only by those with secret wisdom. The chief book is the Zohar, which tells of God as the Infinite One whose ten qualities emanate as powers in the physical world. Adherents stress mystical union of the individual with God and the moral life. Some teach reincarnation.

Reform thought only those parts that agreed with Enlightenment values were inspired), used only Hebrew in their services, forbade instrumental music in worship, separated men and women in the synagogue, and made sure women had their heads covered.

Conservatives, you might say, split the difference. Some have called them "right-wing modernists." Conservatives believed Jewish ritual is the heart and soul of Judaism, but they sympathized with Reform innovations. So they compromised by using mostly Hebrew in their services, some instrumental music, and letting the sexes sit together.

As these movements developed into the twentieth and now twenty-first centuries, Reform and Conservative groups have tended to resemble each other more and more, to the point that by 2007 both movements had agreed to ordain as rabbis sexually active homosexuals and lesbians. It is for this and other reasons that many observers say there are really only two main groups in today's

Judaism—Traditionalists and Modernists. Perhaps the best way to understand today's Judaism is to see how these two camps differ on eight central Jewish ideas: Torah, God, morality, human nature, Israel, religious ritual, the world to come, and Messiah. Milton Steinberg outlined these differences more than fifty years ago in his wonderful book *Basic Judaism*,[2] but the dividing lines are still there today.

Traditionalists and Modernists: The Basic Differences

The best way to see how these two kinds of Jews differ is to look at where they go to find their authority. In other words, how do they answer questions about what is true, good, and beautiful? Traditionalists generally say the answers are found in Torah, while modernists look

> ### Torah
>
> Most of the time when Jews use the word *Torah*, they mean the Pentateuch, the first five books of the Bible (Genesis, Exodus, Leviticus, Numbers, and Deuteronomy). These are the books of Moses.
>
> *Torah* (Hebrew for "guidance" or "teaching") is also used for the totality of teaching by and about God in Judaism. Most Christians are surprised to learn that *Tanakh* (an acronym from the first letters of the Hebrew words for the parts of the Jewish Bible: Torah, Prophets, and Writings), not *Torah*, is the Jewish word for what Christians call the Old Testament.

> ### Bar Mitzvah, Bat Mitzvah, and Confirmation
>
> *Bar mitzvah* is Aramaic for "son of the commandment," and *bat mitzvah* is "daughter of the commandment." Usually these terms refer to the coming-of-age ceremonies for Jewish boys and girls at the ages of thirteen for boys and twelve for girls. This is the age when children are said to be accountable for their sins. At the ceremonies the boy or girl reads or chants parts of the Scriptures in Hebrew and leads in other ways. Many Reform congregations have a confirmation service at about age eighteen, to suggest that the earlier ceremony should be only the beginning of Torah study.

to human reason and experience. For example, to answer the question, What is God like? traditionalists would say they know about God mainly from Torah, while modernists would say that while Torah might have some inspired general ideas about God, such as God's goodness and justice, we need human reason and experience to understand what those abstract ideas mean.

Torah

For traditionalists, every letter and every word in Torah are from God, not only in Torah and the rest of Scripture, but also in the Talmud, which are the rabbinic commentaries that were written in the first through the seventh centuries AD in Babylon (modern Iraq) and Palestine. Traditionalists think that even the rabbinic writings after the Talmud are inspired, but to a diminishing degree of inspiration. Since Torah is God's Word, and God's Word is forever, Judaism should never change—say the traditionalists. Therefore the idea that Judaism has evolved over time is an illusion. People may have changed God's law, but the law itself has not and should not change, for God has revealed his will through the Bible and Jewish tradition, and our task as humans is to stick to it, not change it.

Modernists, on the other hand, say Torah is inspired only in parts—when they find what they consider to be truth and goodness in it. How do they know these parts are good and true? They determine this by using modern reason and experience. The same authorities—modern reason and modern experience—also tell them that the law of change is universal, and therefore Judaism too must change with time. The ancient culture that gave us "revelation" was in fact limited by the cultural mores of those ancient days. Our modern days are blessed with so much more learning and wisdom, and we must use these modern insights to filter out what is ancient and false and bad from what we now see is good and true. That means Judaism must change if it is to continue to be true and good. Torah is revelation but only in some of its broad ideas. Many of its details were not at all inspired but produced by cultures that we had best leave behind.

God

Both traditionalists and modernists say that God is one, not many (against polytheism), not two (against all dualisms, such as

Zoroastrianism or Chinese yin and yang, which believe in two equal forces that fight for mastery of the cosmos), not three (against Christianity, which Jews believe teaches three gods and therefore a kind of polytheism), and not none (against atheism).

Both groups of Jews also agree that the God of the Jewish Bible (and therefore the true God!) is very different from what the religions of the Ancient Near East (ANE)—Babylon, Egypt, Assyria, and Canaan—said about the divine. In other words, the true God is Creator (thus the world had a beginning and is not eternal, as most ANE religions believed), Spirit (God does not have a body, as most ANE religions believed), Lawgiver (God is moral, contrary to the gods of the ANE, who often did immoral things), Guide of history (and thus outside of history, contrary to the ANE gods, who were within history and could do little to change history), and humanity's Helper (using the resources of this world).

On miracles, traditionalists say God still performs them; modernists say God does not, for that would oppose his plan to run the world according to the laws of nature.

Jews and Muslims

Why is there such tension between Jews and Muslims? It is impossible to answer with certainty, but the following factors are involved.

1. Many Muslims believe that Jews stole their birthright by scratching out Ishmael's name and replacing it with Isaac's in the biblical passage where God makes promises to Abraham's progeny (Gen. 21:12). There is no historical evidence for this.

2. The Qur'an praises Jews for being righteous, God-fearing, and humble (3:113–14; 5:82–85; 7:150; 4:162), but it also says they are cowardly, greedy, and treacherous (2:96; 5:13; 5:64; 17:4). Some Jews, it charges, were turned into pigs and apes (2:65; 5:60–61; 7:166).

3. Most Muslims believe Israel unjustly displaced Palestinians from their land in 1948 and continue to oppress them. This is a continuing debate among all those involved; suffice it to say that Israelis also have good claims to the land and have suffered from Palestinian attacks on their citizenry.

4. Middle East historian Bernard Lewis argues that Israel has become a stand-in for Muslim complaints against their own countries, where democracy is rare and the absence of civil liberties prevents them from being heard.

Salvation? Both groups say the word *salvation* may pertain to life after death, but its primary reference is to this world when there is victory over ignorance and selfishness.

Both groups agree that God is both transcendent (separate from this world) and immanent (in the world).

Morality

Traditionalists and modernists both talk about a life of "decency" that is honoring to God. They agree that the prophets in the Hebrew Bible rightly showed us that a life of decency will seek justice and compassion for all human beings. It will perform the mitzvoth (commandments), which are summed up by the Ten Commandments. They forbid idolatry (the first commandment), using God's name irreverently (the second—in the attempt to treat God's name with reverence, many Jews refuse to utter the revealed name "YHWH" and will write "G-d"), dishonoring the Sabbath (third) or parents (fourth), murder (fifth), adultery (sixth), stealing (seventh), lying (eighth), and greed for what others have (ninth and tenth).

Traditionalists believe the moral life is spelled out by the 613 mitzvoth of Torah, while modernists think the general principles of justice and compassion are found through modern reason and experience.

Human Nature

Both traditionalists and modernists believe the human being is free to do what God commands. Here is where Jews and Christians disagree: Jews think the human will is able to master sin if it makes an effort, while Christians believe in original sin, which means the will is disabled by an inherent selfishness that taints all its acts. Jews insist that while we will never be perfect, by repentance we can return to God and use God-given willpower to do what he has told us to do. Christians say this can happen only by the grace of Christ.

Israel

Traditionalists say God chose Israel as the chosen nation because of the merits of the Fathers (Abraham, Isaac, and Jacob), and that Israel (the community of Jews everywhere) now lives to communicate God's truth to the nations.

Rosh Hashanah—Hebrew for "first of the year" or New Year, it comes in September or October. It is a day of judgment, in which one looks at the sins of the past year and reflects on how one should repent and do better the next year. It begins a ten-day penitential season.

Yom Kippur—usually nine days after Rosh Hashanah. This is the most important holiday of the year, the Day of Atonement, when one confesses sins and prays for pardon. This is a day of fasting and services at temple or synagogue. Jews often wear white to symbolize the promise their sins will be made white as snow (Isa. 1:18).

Sukkoth—seven-day feast starting on the fifth day after Yom Kippur, also called Feast of Booths. It marks the forty years that Moses and his people wandered in the desert and lived in booths or tents. Some Jews build a booth in their backyard and eat most or all meals there.

Passover—falls in March or April and marks the greatest event in Jewish history, the exodus of God's people from slavery in Egypt (Exodus 1–15). It lasts seven days (eight outside Israel) and opens the first night with a Seder meal and the retelling of the story of when the angel of death *passed over* the children of Israel. Unleavened bread and bitter herbs are used in the meal to commemorate the exodus events.

Chanukah—in December, it is also called Festival of Lights. It celebrates the taking of the temple back from the Syrian Greeks by the Maccabeans in 142 BC and the miracle of one small cruse of oil, used to rededicate the temple, lasting for eight days.

Purim—also called Feast of Lots, it comes in late February or early March to celebrate God's destruction of Haman, the prime minister in the Persian period (fifth century BC) who cast lots for the slaughter of the Jews. Children make noise whenever Haman's name is mentioned in the liturgy.

This does not mean, by the way, that traditionalists think they are in God's family because of their works. It's more complex and less self-righteous than that. Some decades ago the scholar E. P. Sanders showed that first-century Jews (think especially of the Pharisees) did not think their good works made them members of the kingdom of God. Instead, they believed God had put them into the "covenant" (God's family) by grace, but that they needed to follow the important rules of the Law to *stay* in. Most traditionalists, and also some modernists, believe similarly. They say God made them Jews simply out of his goodness, and now that they are in the covenant, they need to make sure they *stay* in the covenant by obeying God's commandments. This faithfulness ensures a good prospect in the life to come.

Modernists have a different view of chosenness. They agree that the Fathers (Abraham, Isaac, and Jacob) chose God and this is why God chose them. But they add that if other nations choose God, they too will be "chosen." They are a bit embarrassed by the "one chosen nation" idea, and interpret it as a universal call to all nations to observe the divine principles of compassion and justice.

Religious Practices

Traditionalists believe that everything Jews have done in their historic liturgies and daily practices (which have been developed by rabbinic tradition) represents God's will in Torah. Therefore they are scrupulous about even the smallest details, for they believe they are all of God.

Modernists, on the other hand, think the rituals are merely human devices for making us feel close to what is good and divine. These rituals are always subject to improvement, but their basic inspiration may have been divine.

The World to Come

Both groups believe in recompense after death. Goodness on earth will be rewarded then, and evil will be punished. Also both groups affirm immortality and resurrection, but they disagree on what these terms mean. Traditionalists have a more literal conception, and modernists say we can't know anything more precise than the fact of life after death.

In general, Jews think Christians are too presumptuous about immortality and resurrection, and that we really can't guess what the specifics will be like. All we know is that we will survive death and that the life to come will involve the resurrection of the body. No doubt one reason Christians think they know more details about the world to come is that the New Testament teaches far more about these things than does the Old Testament.

Messiah

Traditionalists say the Messiah will be a man, and that they are to hope and pray for the coming of this man. He will not be God, but he will abolish evil and establish goodness on a firm foundation.

The Holocaust

The Holocaust is the period between 1933 and 1945 when German Nazis undertook a systematic destruction of Jewry in Europe. It is estimated that six million Jews were killed. The small-town Jewish community of Eastern Europe was destroyed, and since then Jewish life has centered in Israel and the United States. No Jewish adult can think of faith without also thinking of the Holocaust. Jews cannot separate it from Christian anti-Jewish persecution, which has existed since long before the Middle Ages. Jews have tried to make theological sense of the Holocaust in a variety of ways:

1. Somehow God allowed it in his providence, as he allowed the first two destructions of Jerusalem in 586 BC and AD 70. Perhaps Auschwitz represents Israel as the suffering servant to bring redemption, evidenced in the birth of the state of Israel.
2. Suffering, even on so gargantuan a scale, is punishment for sin.
3. Eliezer Berkowits, Holocaust survivor and theologian: God had to allow such evil because he must allow free will. We are left like Job, believing in a God beyond understanding.
4. Emil Fackenheim, Jewish philosopher: God was somehow present, but we must not hand Hitler a posthumous victory by failing to survive or remember or despair.
5. Richard Rubenstein, Jewish scholar: God, as the One on whom we depend, is dead. God is a different God.
6. Elie Wiesel, Holocaust survivor and eminent novelist and Nobel laureate: Humans are on their own. Israel is too convenient to be an answer to the Holocaust. We are thrown into an abyss of non-meaning. We need a new covenant because the old one was broken, but not by us. The presence of God is found in a silent and enigmatic tear.

Modernists, in contrast, are looking not to a man but to an age—a messianic age. But God is not the primary mover here. We human beings will bring it about by working for our dreams of justice and goodness. God inspires our dreams, and Torah helps us understand them, but it will be our efforts that will bring this age to pass.

Perhaps you are wondering why Jews say the Messiah will not be God. This is because Jews observe that the Old Testament prophecies never predict that the Messiah will be God. Christians point to Isaiah 9:6: "For a child has been born for us . . . and he is named Wonderful Counselor, Mighty God," but Jews translate this as referring not to Messiah but to God who sent this child: "For a child has been born to us, a son has been given us. And authority has settled on his shoulders. He has been named 'The Mighty God is planning grace; the Eternal Father, a peaceable ruler'" (Jewish Publication Society Tanakh).

Christians see Jesus as God not so much because of prophecies in the Old Testament but because of what they see in his life. For example, he claimed the authority to forgive sins, which all first-century Jews knew was the prerogative of God alone (Mark 2:7). This by itself, completely apart from his miracles, was Jesus' own claim to divinity.

The primary reason Jews don't think Jesus was the anticipated Messiah is that he did not bring worldwide peace and submission of the nations to himself, as the psalmist and prophets said he would (Ps. 2:9; Isa. 9:2–7; 11:1–5; Jer. 33:14–26; Ezek. 37:24–28). Quite the opposite, his followers caused division and conflict in first-century Israel, and representatives of the greatest king, Caesar, had him put to death.

Christians reply that there are two streams of prophecy in *Tanakh* (the Old Testament) about the Messiah. Indeed, one says he will bring worldwide peace and justice, but there is another one that suggests the Messiah will be a suffering Servant whose sufferings will save the world (Psalms 22, 55, 88; Isa. 53:5, 10, 12; see also Exod. 32:32, where Moses prefigures the willingness of One who suffers to save others). Jesus suffered and saved in his first coming and will bring worldwide peace and justice in his second.

Jacob Neusner, a Jewish scholar, published the book *A Rabbi Talks with Jesus*[3] in which he said he cannot accept Jesus as Messiah because a true Jew would never reject the Jewish law, which was the greatest gift God gave to his people. Neusner says Jesus changed the law and focused not on daily holiness (which the law is all about) but on an individual's salvation in the next life.

Christians say that Jesus did not reject biblical law but taught the true meaning of the law. In fact he took the law very seriously, as these words in the Sermon on the Mount show:

> Do not think that I have come to abolish the Law or the Prophets; I have come not to abolish them but to fulfill them. For truly, I say to you, until heaven and earth pass away, not an iota, not a dot, will

Hasidism

Hasidism, from the Hebrew word for "pietist," is a movement stemming from the massacre of Jews in the Crusades and new massacres in seventeenth-century Eastern Europe. The adherents repudiated an earlier asceticism and adopted mystical elements, including Kabbalah, teaching that true redemption is found in the internal religious spirit of each individual. Hasidism places great importance on the spiritual leader, the zaddik or righteous man, who is seen as a ladder between heaven and earth. Huge numbers of Hasidic Jews perished in the Holocaust, but the movement is reviving in Israel and the United States. It is staunchly Orthodox but takes a variety of social positions, from affirmation to denial of the world and from Zionism to anti-Zionism.

Talmud

The Talmud is the written collection of Jewish oral tradition and commentaries on that tradition. Orthodox Jews believe God told Moses orally how to interpret and apply the written law. Moses passed this oral tradition down to the rabbis, who developed it until the end of the second century AD, when it was written down. This was the Mishnah. Then for the next three centuries rabbis in Jerusalem and Babylon commented in writing on the Mishnah in a series of books known as the Gemara. The combination of Mishnah and Gemara is the Talmud.

pass from the Law until all is accomplished. Therefore whoever relaxes one of the least of these commandments and teaches others to do the same will be called least in the kingdom of heaven, but whoever does them and teaches them will be called great in the kingdom of heaven.

Matthew 5:17–19 ESV

David Gelernter is a Jewish computer scientist at Yale who also writes widely respected books and articles on theology and politics. Reflecting the thinking of some fellow Jews, he has said that he cannot accept Christian faith, and Jesus' claims at the center of it, because of Jesus' incipient pacifism. "Turn the other cheek" and "Do not resist the evildoer" are teachings that cannot support a robust resistance to evil, which this age of terrorism demands.

Yet most Christians throughout history have supported the just war tradition, which is based on New Testament teachings. They believe there are times when Christians can and must fight wars to resist evil. They look to passages such as Romans 13:4 ("the authority does not bear the sword in vain!") and say Jesus' admonition not to resist the evildoer (Matt. 5:39) was probably a restatement of Psalm 37:1 ("Do not fret because of the wicked"), not a sign of pacifism.

But even if Jews do not agree on who Jesus is, we Christians must always remember that they are our older brothers and sisters. Without them, we wouldn't be here. God chose to bring us to faith only through their faith and one of their sons.

Buddhism

The West's Favorite Non-Christian Religion

Buddhism is popular among college students today. I think there are a number of reasons for this. One is that the Buddha's search for truth and his willingness to forsake the world strike chords in young seekers who recognize the emptiness of materialism. It is also attractive to those who have been turned off by Christianity, for one reason or another, and want some sort of spiritual alternative.

Facts on the Ground

Let's start, as we did in the last chapter, with numbers and places. How many Buddhists are there, and where do they live?

In 2007 there were 386 million Buddhists, or 6 percent of the world's population. Estimates of the number of Buddhists in the United States range from 1.5 to 2 million, with 75–80 percent being Asian.

Those who follow Theravada, which is the school of Buddhism closest to the teachings of Gautama Buddha, the founder, are located primarily in Southeast Asia: Sri Lanka, Myanmar, Cambodia, and Thailand. The Mahayana school, which may have started later in China and became more popular, is prevalent in China and East Asia (Japan and Korea). Zen Buddhism was started in Japan and has spread west, while Tibetan Buddhism is of course centered in that mountainous land bordering China but has become popular around the world because of the Dalai Lama's attractive persona and teaching.

The Story of the Buddha

Siddhartha Gautama Buddha (ca. 448–368 BC) grew up in the lap of luxury. He was the son of a king in the mountain fastnesses of what is now Nepal. Not unnaturally, he was indulged by his father. But Gautama's environment went far beyond what we would imagine. Apparently in an attempt to protect his son from the harsh realities of life, Gautama's father made sure the boy never saw the suffering and deprivation of old age, disease, and death. It's hard to imagine how Gautama could grow up never having seen or known of death, but that is how the story goes.

At some point in Gautama's twenties, reality broke through. On the first of several chariot rides, Gautama saw an old man. "Oh no!" he exclaimed. "Do you mean I will someday suffer like that?"

Then on a second chariot ride, he saw a sick person who was obviously in pain. This opened his eyes to the pervasiveness of suffering in the world. Gautama was sorely distressed.

A third chariot ride brought the sight of a corpse in a funeral procession. This too alarmed Gautama. "What? We don't live forever?" The young man sunk into despair. Life seemed hopeless.

But then there was another sight sometime later that brought him hope. This time he saw a figure on the horizon walking in a saffron robe. It was probably a Hindu sannyasi, a holy man who was practicing asceticism and meditation in the quest of *moksha* (liberation from the cycle of reincarnation).

"Who is that?" he asked his driver.

"Oh, he's seeking the way beyond life and death," he was told. That meant that this Hindu seeker was trying to reach the state where he would not be reborn into another life in this world but be joined with Brahman, the impersonal Absolute (see chapter 1). For Gautama, this meant there might be a way to avoid the suffering of life and death.

By this time in his life, Gautama was married and had a son, but the Four Sights (of age, disease, death, and the way beyond death) made him reconsider his direction in life. At the age of twenty-nine he decided he would follow the way of the sannyasi

The Fourteenth Dalai Lama

Dalai lama means, literally, "guru [as big as the] ocean," or more colloquially, "spiritual teacher." Many (not all) Tibetan Buddhists believe the current Dalai Lama, Tenzin Gyatso (1935–), is the reincarnation of a bodhisattva who was once a disciple of Gautama and then took a special interest in Tibet. The winner of the Nobel Peace Prize, he is the leader of the Gelug school of Tibetan Buddhism, and is thought to be the highest lama among the several Tibetan schools.

In his book *The Art of Happiness*,[1] the Dalai Lama asserts that happiness can be found by training the mind. We can do things like loving our enemies by thinking of what we have in common with them (desire for happiness, physical bodies, birth, death) and their good qualities. We suffer because we think we are at the center of the world. Instead, we should be altruistic and have compassion, because these qualities will make us stronger and healthier.

he had seen. Gautama left his wife and son and set off into the wilderness.

Some explanation is needed here: back then it was a religious tradition to leave one's family to seek enlightenment, and he left his wife and son with his extended family. They probably believed this would give them good karma (literally "deeds," which would help produce a better reincarnation). But we are also told that his wife was angry with him for leaving them. This departure is called the Great Renunciation.

Gautama went all the way in following what the Hindu traditions were telling him then—practice asceticism and meditate until you are enlightened. He embraced this new life so radically that he was reduced to skin and bones. We're told that when he put his hand on his stomach, he could feel his backbone.

But it didn't work. Enlightenment never came.

So Gautama decided he would demand results. He would sit under a tree (later it became known as the *bodhi* or enlightenment tree) until revelation came.

He sat all day and evening and night until finally enlightenment came. During the early morning hours, he was given revelation after revelation after revelation. He saw all the truths of reality, which he would teach for the next fifty-odd years until his death from food poisoning. He had come to be free of all desire and so achieved, after this one night, nirvana (literally, the "blowing out" of desire).

The Buddha's Teachings

That night the Buddha (now we can use this title, for it refers to his enlightened knowledge) saw what Buddhists have called ever since the Four Noble Truths.

The First Noble Truth

The first Noble Truth is that *all is suffering*. This doesn't mean that every minute of the day we feel bad. It means something Christians can understand: that at the deepest level, all of life is dissatisfactory. Even when we're having fun and being successful, we know deep inside that there is something missing—if we haven't found spiritual reality.

The Second Noble Truth

The second Noble Truth is that *the cause of suffering is desire*. The Buddha said there are three desires that humans feel: desire for sensual pleasure, desire for becoming someone recognized and esteemed, and desire for nonbecoming or suicide. He recognized that most of us do not feel the third desire most of the time.

The Buddha said there is a reason we are filled with these desires: our ignorance. We saw in the first chapter that Hindus also feel ignorance is our central problem, but while Hindus feel we are ignorant of Brahman or a personal god, Gautama Buddha said we are ignorant of the Three Characteristics of Existence.

The first is *impermanence*. This means that nothing ever remains the same, even Brahman, which was the philosophical Hindu idea

The Four Noble Truths

1. All is suffering.
2. Suffering is caused by desire.
3. The way to be rid of suffering is to be rid of desire.
4. The way to be rid of desire is to follow the Noble Eightfold Path.

The Three Characteristics of Existence

1. Impermanence
2. Suffering
3. No self

of ultimate reality. Hindus said this is the only unchanging reality. But the Buddha rejected this. He said nothing is permanent; everything is constantly changing. This also meant there is no unchanging substance behind and within anything in the cosmos, so nothing has independent existence.

Christians can agree with this in part, for they say that nothing exists apart from God. There is nothing that exists on its own. But the Buddha rejected the idea of a creator God who is responsible for all things. He said there are gods, but they are not creators and certainly not redeemers, and they need to attain the same enlightenment you and I do. So, for all practical purposes, the Buddha was an agnostic. He said he didn't know if there was a supreme God, which is what "agnostic" means—"I do not know." In any event, he did not believe in a God who created the world and now controls it. And he looked not to a god but to his own self for any sort of "salvation."

The second characteristic of existence is *suffering*, which we have already seen is the first Noble Truth. The third is that *there is no self*. This follows from the first characteristic, that everything is impermanent. Let me try to explain.

If there is nothing permanent in Jane, let's say, then there can't be anything that remains the same from year to year, month to month, or even moment to moment. Can that be? Well, we know that our atoms and cells are constantly changing, so at the level of the body, that must be true—there is nothing permanent.

What about Jane's mind? Her thoughts are constantly changing, especially as she experiences new things, which she does during her waking hours and when she is dreaming. If her experiences are constantly giving her new perspectives, how can her mind remain the same? You say her basic attitudes are the same? But how can they be? If her perspective is constantly changing (even if minutely) because of her new experiences, then even her attitudes change with an ever-changing perspective. They may not change much but they change nevertheless.

If Jane's mind and body are constantly changing, we'd have to say the same about her emotions and will. As life brings new things, good and bad, her feelings go up and down. And her desires, expressed by her will, will also change as these feelings change.

If Jane's mind, body, feelings, and will continually change, then there can't be anything about her that remains the same. And what is the self but the combination of mind, body, feelings, and will? Therefore Buddhists say Jane has no self—at least one that remains the same across time.

By the way, the Buddha said that as long as we think we have a permanent self, we will be all the more attached to this self and unable to give up desire—which keeps us suffering and stuck in samsara, the endless cycle of reincarnation. So knowing that we have no permanent self is part of our liberation. It helps us get rid of desire, which in turn helps us attain nirvana (more on that in a bit).

How Can There Be Reincarnation If There Is No Self?

Buddhists give three answers to the oft-asked question, How can there be reincarnation if there is no self?

1. The Buddha didn't answer the question, but he did say, according to tradition, "This is my last birth." So he was able to keep the two together.
2. The people believe in both reincarnation and no self, and that's the important thing. Like much of life, two seemingly incompatible things hold together because they are both true. Think of the nature of light—it is both a particle and a wave.
3. The deeds cause the existence of another person. The fire that is passed from one torch to another creates a new fire, and yet it is from the original fire. So too our deeds: there is a "causal connection" between the first and second flames, but they are now separate, and so there is no enduring, single flame.

The Noble Eightfold Path

1. Right understanding
2. Right thinking
3. Right speech
4. Right action
5. Right livelihood
6. Right effort
7. Right mindfulness
8. Right concentration

The Third Noble Truth

Let's take stock of what we have learned so far about the Buddha's teaching. All is suffering (the first Noble Truth), the cause of suffering is desire (the second Noble Truth), which comes from ignorance of the Three Characteristics of Existence. Now we must go on to the third Noble Truth: *the way to be rid of suffering is to be rid of desire.* The eventual "blowing out" of desire is nirvana, which is a state of cessation of suffering that can be experienced at one level in this life and at another level after death.

The nirvana in this life is called "nirvana with remainder," and in the next life it is "nirvana without remainder." The "remainder" refers to karma, which are deeds that keep us in this cycle of reincarnation (samsara). Nirvana in the next life, without remainder, is nothing like anything we can imagine. In fact the Buddha taught that in nirvana there are no desires, thoughts, or beings. So we have to say that nirvana is the end of human existence as we know it. Perhaps it is like that drop of water I described in the first chapter that hits the surface of the ocean and in a matter of milliseconds no longer exists as an individual drop. Its contents have dispersed and merged with the ocean. The "I" is no longer a being (of course it never was a self anyway!), but that's not the important thing for the Buddha. The important thing is that suffering is over, which is the goal of the Buddha's teaching.

The Fourth Noble Truth

The fourth Noble Truth is this: *the way to be rid of desire is to follow the Noble Eightfold Path.* The first step on that path is *right understanding*. This means proper understanding of the Buddha's teachings, such as the Four Noble Truths and the Three Characteristics of Existence. Don't believe anyone who says something like the following: "In Buddhism (as opposed to Christianity) it doesn't matter what you believe; all that matters is what you do."

You can see from this first step on the Noble Eightfold Path that it matters very much what you believe. If you do not believe what the Buddha taught about suffering and the self, for example, you will not make it past square one in Buddhism.

The second step is *right thinking*, which involves thinking about truth (the Buddha's teachings again) and not how to build up your own self, for that just increases desire. The third step is *right speech*, which means no lying or slander or gossip. *Right action* (the fourth step) means following the Five Precepts: no killing, stealing, sexual sin, lying, or alcohol. Let me explain some of these.

No killing means just that—the taking of life, even animal life, is forbidden. So consistent Buddhists are vegetarians and pacifists. That does not mean that Buddhists never eat meat or fight in war, any more than that Christians have always forgiven their enemies. But those are the ideals.

Sexual sin means sin outside of marriage for laity, and any sex at all for Buddhist monks and nuns. Notice, by the way, that

Worshiping Amitabha Buddha

I believe that in the remotest west of this miserable world there is a world where only happiness exists. Here there is no place for suffering. As long as I have a devout belief in, and devotedly chant the name of, the Buddha of that world—Amitabha Buddha—I am definitely bound to get to that world in my next life. Therefore I chant "Nan Wu Amitabha Buddha" every morning as soon as I get up, before and after meals, and whenever I encounter both joyful things and sorrowful things. Wherever I go and am, as long as I meet believers in Amitabha, I always chant the Buddha's name before I speak to that believer. Whenever I make a phone call to a Buddhist, my first word is the Amitabha chant. On the first and fifteenth day of each month in the Chinese lunar calendar, I burn incense and worship the Buddha image enshrined in my house. On those days I chant his name at least one thousand times.

A man in northwest China

Buddhist ethics are very similar to Christian moral rules. The same is true for the other major religions. Christians differ on application and interpretation, but the same basic principles—actually, those of the Ten Commandments—are taught by all the great religions. As C. S. Lewis once said, if you went to the British Museum (which is a library) to research the moral teachings of the great civilizations, you'd get bored after three days, for they all say nearly the same things. He pointed this out in "Illustrations of the Tao," the appendix to his book *The Abolition of Man*.[2]

Right action (the fourth step on the Noble Path) also includes the Four Unlimited Virtues (friendliness, compassion, sympathetic joy, and even-mindedness). The last virtue means remaining even-keeled even in times of suffering and joy. This, Buddhists say, is possible only after meditation.

The fifth step is *right livelihood*. That means some occupations are obviously forbidden to the faithful Buddhist: arms sales, butchering animals, producing intoxicants, for example.

The last three steps (*right effort, right mindfulness,* and *right concentration*) all have to do with meditation, which is the Buddhist way par excellence to spiritual advancement.

Theravada

There are four main schools of Buddhism—Theravada, Mahayana, Zen, and Tibetan. I will discuss the first two, which are the largest, in the next two sections (see sidebars for brief descriptions of Zen and Tibetan Buddhism).

Theravada, which is Pali for the "Way of the Elders," took most of its present shape by the second century BC, about two centuries after the death of the Buddha. Of the four schools just mentioned, it is probably closest to what historians think Gautama actually taught.

Its chief goal is liberation from samsara in nirvana, which, as we saw earlier in this chapter, is the end of consciousness and individuality. The Theravada school regards the gods as real but unhelpful in the human search to end suffering. It says the human self is unreal, and lives many lives in many heavens and hells before it reaches nirvana, since most of us are not spiritual enough to have attained nirvana before the end of one life. And it says the world is not a thing but a process, with no beginning or end. Remember here the Buddha's teaching that nothing is permanent and standing on its own. This is also true for the world.

According to Theravada, the basic human problem is suffering in samsara because of ignorance of the Buddha's teachings. That ignorance creates desire, which in turn is responsible for our suffering. The resolution to our problem(s) is to accept what the Buddha taught and practice his virtues and precepts.

Some have asked how this can be a religion, for it doesn't have the

Zen Buddhism

Zen is the Japanese derivation from a Sanskrit word meaning "meditation." It started in China, moved to Japan, and uses meditation techniques to achieve *satori* (enlightenment). It de-emphasizes the use of Buddhist scriptures and philosophy and points more to direct experience. Zen teaches that ultimate reality is beyond ordinary words and thinking and so uses verbal paradoxes and intense meditation to set the mind free to see the beyond. Zen is associated with tea ceremonies, haiku, and even swordsmanship, because adherents rely on images rather than words and seek naturalness not formality.

Buddhist Monks

In countries dominated by Theravada Buddhism, the monastery (*sangha*) is the center of Buddhist life. Laity come once a week to hear teaching and give offerings, including food for the monks. Monks (*bhikkus*) eat once a day, not after noon, often after walking single file through the streets in silence and with their eyes on the ground, collecting alms. Laymen and laywomen believe that by giving offerings they are building merit or good karma that will help them achieve a better rebirth in the next life.

Mantras, Mudras, and Mandalas

Mantras are ritual formulas or sounds used to help one focus in meditation. In Mahayana Buddhism they are used to invoke a deity or gain protection.

Mudras are hand gestures used along with certain postures to aid meditation.

Mandalas are diagrams or pictures, often circular, used in meditation; some Buddhists use them to visualize the Buddha's qualities.

earmarks of what most of us think of when we hear the word *religion*. There is no worship, for there is no god who made us or the world or who will save us. Neither are there prayer, praise, forgiveness, or heaven. Judgment and a final hell are missing. The Buddha was always silent about the future life, except to say what it is not—a place of beings, consciousness, or desire.

But in another sense this is a religion. It is a complete way of thinking and practice that answers (or at least struggles with) the most important questions in life: Who or what are we? Where did we come from? Where are we going? How should we live our lives?

In this sense, of course, even atheism is a religion, for it too answers these questions.

This may seem odd to you, to call atheism and this kind of Buddhism "religions" when their adherents don't believe in God. But it does help explain how Theravada (and other) Buddhists can feel religious and look toward reality with reverence without believing in a personal god.

Mahayana

The first Mahayana (Sanskrit for "Great Vehicle," which suggests it carries many more souls than its rival Theravada) *Sutras* (scriptures) were written between the first and eighth centuries AD. In them you can see distinct departures from Theravada positions. Here are the most important differences.

Tibetan Buddhism

While Theravada says there are no living Buddhas today, and Mahayana says there are no Buddhas now on earth except in other dimensions, Tibetans emphasize the experience of real Buddhas dwelling among us. They believe Padma Sambhava, an early Buddha who lived at about the same time as Gautama, visited Tibet in the twelfth century of his life and is still alive in a hidden paradise near Madagascar. Tibetan Buddhism emphasizes the use of a mentor or *lama*. The purpose of life, it says, is to transcend the ego-centered animal life to become a Buddha and share with the infinite numbers of other Buddhas.

The Chinese government has killed one million Tibetans and destroyed all but 13 of its 6,267 monasteries. Some Tibetans believe this is a sign that the golden age is near. Many (not all) Tibetan Buddhists believe the current Dalai Lama is the reincarnation of a bodhisattva (Sanskrit for "a being for enlightenment") who was once a disciple of Gautama and then took a special interest in Tibet.

1. *Universalism.* Whereas in Theravada male monks have been the only ones considered spiritual enough to attain nirvana, Mahayana promises the possibility of liberation for everyone.
2. *Fast and easy.* In Theravada liberation takes many lives (in samsara, the reincarnation process), but Mahayana promises liberation after only one life. And it doesn't take lengthy, rigorous meditation—in some Mahayana schools, if you simply look with sincere faith one time during your life to the Buddha, you will escape samsara after death. It's no wonder Mahayana is the largest and most popular segment of Buddhism.

3. *Buddha as god.* While Theravada teaches that the Buddha was just a man, Mahayana talks about the divine Buddha, and de-emphasizes the historical Gautama.

4. *Many Buddhas.* Theravada focuses on the one Buddha in history, Gautama. But Mahayanists speak of an infinite number of Buddhas. And Mahayana teachers also say each one of us has a latent Buddha nature, so that we are all unrealized Buddhas.

5. *Grace.* The Mahayana ideal figure is the bodhisattva who was on his way to Buddhahood but stopped to help those still ignorant and suffering in samsara. The bodhisattva is said to have one foot in our world and one in nirvana. He keeps the one foot here so that he can impart grace to those who need it. The most important bodhisattva is Amitabha (in Japan, Amida), who in the distant past said he would bring to his Pure Land all who called on his name in faith. He forgives their sins because of their faith and saves them from more lives in samsara. Strictly speaking, however, these bodhisattvas are already Buddhas.

6. *Levels of truth.* Like Shankara (see the first chapter on Hinduisms), Mahayana Buddhists talk about levels of reality and truth. The earthly Buddha, Gautama, is at the lowest level. Above that level are the paradisal heavens that are full of Buddhas and bodhisattvas. Each one of the latter is a bodily form of what they call "absolute Buddha nature." Then at the highest level is the ultimate nature of reality, which is nirvana. This is non-dual, which means that there are no distinctions in it. All is one. Nothing separates anything from anything else. There are no individuals here. What we think of as the human self is lost in the ocean of the ultimate Oneness, like the drop of water that hits the surface of the ocean.

Christian Analysis

I think you can see that Jesus and the Buddha were very different. The most important difference is that the Buddha did not believe in a God as we know him (Buddha was agnostic on that) and certainly didn't know the triune God. Later Mahayana traditions came to believe in deities known as Buddhas and bodhisattvas, but Gautama Buddha said that he was no more than a man and that there is no creator or divine being who can help us achieve our spiritual goals. This is why Sakyamuni, as the original Buddha is known by many Buddhists, said that we are to be lamps unto ourselves. In contrast, Jesus said that he was the light of the world.

> **Mahayana**
>
> 1. Ultimate concern: rebirth in the Pure Land of Amitabha Buddha or becoming a Buddha
> 2. View of reality:
>   a. Gods: many bodhisattvas and Buddhas
>   b. Self: none in theory but yes in practice
>   c. World: either impermanent or (for some Mahayanist philosophers) unreal
> 3. Basic human problem: suffering in samsara because of ignorance of Amitabha Buddha or absolute Buddha nature
> 4. Resolution:
>   a. Pure Land school: call in faith on Amitabha Buddha
>   b. Other philosophical schools: lose attachment to all theories or meditate with the realization that all that exists is finally only pure thought

We Christians say that we are not on our own, as the Buddha suggested, but can ask for the grace of Jesus to do for us what we cannot do. While Jesus emphasized moral corruption as the heart of the basic human problem (Mark 7:20–23), the Buddha said desire—for gratification of one's senses and one's ego—is the root of all suffering. With love one can become a bodhisattva, but only knowledge enables one to become a Buddha. Perhaps as a result, Buddhist and Christian portrayals of the spiritual ideal are curiously different: Buddhists look to a smiling Buddha seated on a lotus blossom, while Christians worship a suffering Jesus nailed to a cross. The Buddha taught his followers to escape suffering, while Jesus showed a way to conquer suffering by embracing it.

Although Buddhist and Christian ethics agree on important principles (that stealing, lying, the killing of innocent life, and sexual misconduct are wrong, and that compassion and sympathy are imperative), they differ on the relationship of ethics to ultimate reality. For Gautama Buddha and Theravadins, the ethical life is a provisional raft that takes us to the other shore of nirvana where it can then be discarded, for in nirvana differences between good and evil no longer exist. But for Christians, the distinction between right and wrong is part of the fabric of reality and will persist into eternity.

Ethical differences extend to relations between the sexes. In early Buddhism particularly you find the idea that you can become a Buddha only if you are reborn in the form of a man. Not until much later did Mahayanists accept female bodhisattvas. Buddhist monasteries today dominate Theravadin life, but most orders for nuns disappeared centuries ago. While Christian history contains plenty of sexism, Jesus himself never demonized women or sexuality. When compared to the rigid structure of Buddhist monasticism, which is at the heart of Theravada, Jesus' circle of disciples appears casual and free.

Buddhists and Christians look at ethics differently, in large part because they regard history in radically different ways. Buddhists read in the *Dhammapada* (a Buddhist scripture) that "there is no misery like physical existence" (15.6). Earthly existence is necessarily a vale of tears because as long as one remains in the endless cycle of life, death, and rebirth, suffering is inevitable. The desire, which life in this world produces, always brings suffering. We're told we can escape suffering only by escaping this wearisome cycle of rebirth. So we have to break ties to this world and its routines, particularly family life and sexuality.

Jesus, however, never spoke harsh words about sexual relationship. He announced a salvation that comes not by renouncing life in the world but by a trust that is lived out in loving commitment amid the everyday routines of worldly life. According to him, marriage is not an impediment to spirituality but the ordinary realm in which salvation is lived out. Abstention from family life and sexuality is an option, but not a higher path for the spiritual elite.

At the same time I should say that this contrast should not be drawn too sharply. Christian monasticism has at times been just as world-denying as its Buddhist counterpart. Beginning with the apostle Paul (1 Corinthians 7), there have been many Christians who have concluded that they could find God best apart from family and sexuality. And while monasticism has been more integral to Theravada than to Christianity, Jesus himself chose not to marry or regard family as the center of the spiritual life (Matt. 10:37; 12:49–50), and the vast majority of Buddhists enjoy the fullness of married life and participation in the secular world.

There's one final difference between Buddhism and

The Japanese Pure Land school of Mahayana Buddhism contains an extraordinary example of grace outside of Christianity. Shinran (1173–1262), the founder of Jodo Shinshu (Pure Land True Sect), rejected all "ways of effort" in the search for salvation and preached that we must rely on "the power of the other," which for him was Amida Buddha, who would bring to his Pure Land all those who have faith in his power. Shinran's conviction of underlying sin in all human beings is reminiscent of Paul or Augustine:

> In their outward seeming are all men diligent and truth speaking,
> But in their souls are greed and anger and unjust deceitfulness.
> And in their flesh do lying and cunning triumph.

His despair over the inner corruption of even his outward righteousness seems to be an Asian translation of Isaiah:

> Even my righteous deeds, being mingled with this poison, must be named the deeds of deceitfulness. . . . I, whose mind is filled with cunning and deceit as the poison of reptiles, am impotent to practice righteous deeds.

And his hope for divine mercy reads like a line from Martin Luther:

> There is no mercy in my soul. The good of my fellow man is not dear in mine eyes.
> If it were not for the Ark of Mercy,
> The divine promise of the Infinite Wisdom,
> How should I cross the Ocean of Misery?[3]

Christianity, and one of the most important: hope. If you are following the teachings of the original Buddha—Siddhartha Gautama—you have little or no hope for life after death. Sure, you can hope for nirvana, but this is a realm in which "you" are no longer a "you." There is no individual self there in which to enjoy freedom from suffering.

However, Jesus gives us the promise of eternal life as an individual self joined to him and the Father and the Spirit, in fellowship with the millions and perhaps billions of other saints—not only family and friends but the great souls throughout history. And that fellowship, with joy and learning, will continue through all eternity, because there is an infinite number of things and persons for us to see and enjoy.

The contrast is more than enormous.

Confucianism and Daoism

Two of the Biggest Nation's Three Religions

Scholars often refer to the "three religions of China," by which they mean Confucianism, Daoism, and Buddhism. This doesn't mean that there are three groups of Chinese, with each group following one of the three religions. No, the Chinese tend not to be exclusive in their religions, which means they usually don't adhere to one and only one. Most Chinese have some devotion to all three of these religions. So in reality, these are not so much three distinct religions for the Chinese but three elements of one religious whole.

Some have said that for mysticism (experiencing the divine realm directly) Chinese go to Daoism, for morals they go to Confucianism, and for after-death needs they go to Buddhism. There is another element in the religious lives of most Chinese that is not among "the big three" but is important nonetheless, and that's spiritism—giving reverence to the spirits of their ancestors. Since it is not among the major world religions, we won't go more deeply into it. For more on this subject, check out *Christianity and Chinese Religions* by Hans Küng and Julia Ching.

You could also say that many Chinese wear a Confucianist hat for everyday life, Daoist robes for religious ceremonies, and Buddhist sandals for stepping into the next life. One scholar has written, "Daoism is the playing mood of the Chinese people, Confucianism is their working mood, and Buddhism is their eschatological [dealing with the end of life] mood."

Of course the religions of the Chinese are not that simple. Besides those who follow Confucianism, Daoism, and Buddhism, there are 80–100 million Chinese Christians and at least 50 million Muslims in China. (In fact China may have more active Christians than any other country in the world!) But the fact remains that in this most populous nation of the world (1.3 billion in July 2007), the majority would affirm the three-religion mix: Confucianism-Daoism-Buddhism, with ancestor reverence/worship thrown in for good measure.

In the last chapter we looked at Buddhism, so we don't need to say anything more about that piece of the Chinese religious pie here. The rest of this chapter will focus on Confucianism and Daoism.

Confucianism

Confucius (Master Kong, as the Chinese called him) was born in 551 BC in what is now the Shantung province of north China, just across the Yellow Sea from Korea. His ancestors had been men of importance in politics and literature. His father, who was a distinguished soldier, died when Confucius was only three.

In the first period of his career Confucius was a well-known teacher of Chinese ritual and the art of government. Many young men are said to have come to study with him. His public service didn't start until he was fifty. Two years later he was made Minister of Justice in the state of Chengdu, where he improved manners and morals, strengthening the hand of its leader. When this leader rejected Confucius' advice to decline an offer of horses and dancing girls from a neighboring prince, Confucius resigned in disgust. He left with a handful of students and wandered as a teacher from state to state. After fourteen years as an itinerant teacher, he died at the age of seventy-three.

Confucius is famous for many things. He was the first to offer a school for all young men, regardless of their status or means. In his *Analects* he wrote, "In education, there should be no class distinction" (15.38). This applied, however, only to males.

He is also responsible for the six Confucian Classics—the Books of Changes, Poetry, History, Rituals, Music, and Spring and Autumn Annals. But rather than writing these from scratch, he organized and edited them so they could be passed down to later generations.

Confucian Teachings

Confucius was an innovative thinker, and his moral and religious teachings have shaped the Chinese mind for thousands of years—even during the darkest years of Chinese Communism when Mao Zedong (you may be familiar with the older spelling Mao Tse-tung) tried to eradicate his influence. Mao's mad, murderous Red Guards during the Cultural Revolution (1965–75) drove Confucius' followers and his legacy underground. But in the 1990s, when China's Communist leaders realized that such a moral vacuum creates madness, they opened the door for Confucianism to reemerge. Now, like before, its influence is everywhere in China. If modern Chinese aren't familiar with Confucian teachers explicitly because of earlier Communist efforts, they have nevertheless picked up by osmosis the Confucian emphasis on reverence for elders and ancestors and dedication to education.

Many have said Confucius taught only ethics not religion. But while it is true that Confucius was primarily a moralist, he was no secular humanist (saying there is no divine realm, only humanity). He said, "Heaven has appointed me to teach this doctrine." So he felt called by heaven to teach his philosophy of life. *Heaven* was his term for the realm of the divine. He also believed in prayer—that heaven answers prayer—and was convinced that "Heaven punishes evil and rewards good."

So Confucianism, as taught by Master Kong (remember, this is Confucius), was a kind of humanism, but neither secular nor self-sufficient. It was a religious humanism.

The central thesis of this religious humanism was what Confucius called *jen*, best translated "benevolence." It is formed in Chinese by two characters—one meaning "human being," and the other meaning "two." The combination of the characters has been translated as both "righteousness" and "benevolence," referring to unself-conscious efforts for the good of others. Think here of the Good Samaritan, who did not think of himself and reasons not to help the half-dead Jew but thought only of what that poor Jew needed—healing and a place to rest. That Samaritan, who might have been despised by the Jew before the Jew had been beaten unconscious, was practicing *jen*.

Confucius and his successors taught single-minded devotion to virtue. They found joy in following what he called the *Dao* (literally, "the Way") even when it means poverty, suffering, and death. They said righteous people would be happy eating coarse rice and drinking water if necessary to follow the Way, because they were interested in doing what is right, not in making a profit. They didn't worry about getting a full belly or a comfortable home but whether they were being true to the Way.

Therefore virtuous people never abandon righteousness (*yi*) in adversity and do not depart from the Way in success. They refuse to remain in wealth or a prestigious position if either

was gained in a wrong manner. Even for one basketful of rice, they would not bend. If it had been necessary to perpetrate one wrong deed or kill one innocent person to gain the empire, no virtuous person would consent to doing either. True virtue (*te*) is being unconcerned with what others think and recognizing that it is better to be disliked by bad people than to be liked by all. With *te* one is ready to give up even life itself if that is necessary to follow the way of benevolence.

When Confucius was traveling in southern China and his disciples realized that their master would never again have an opportunity to put his principles into practice (as a minister of state), they wanted to know how he felt. They asked him about two ancient sages who under bad kings had died of starvation. Confucius replied that they were true men—something he rarely said of anyone past or present. So a disciple asked him again, "Do you think they had any regrets?" Confucius responded firmly, "Why, they wanted *jen* (benevolence), and they achieved it. Why should they regret it?"

While we moderns might find this ideal both admirable and frightening, Confucius and his disciple Mencius (372–289 BC) found it a source of joy. In the *Analects* Confucius often remarks on the joy he finds in *jen* and *yi*, even when deprived of what we would call necessities of life. One can have joy, he said, living on a bowlful of rice and a ladleful of water in a run-down hut. "In the

I think somewhere in the universe there is a supreme God called Heaven, who is watching us at every moment and will reward good and punish evil. I don't worship Heaven in a concrete way, or keep Heaven in my heart constantly, but whenever I consider doing something indecent, I stop for fear of possible punishment from Heaven. Whenever I have a good fortune or something happy, I thank Heaven for its grace. On August 27 every year in the Chinese lunar calendar, we celebrate the day of Confucius' birth. On this day we have a grand memorial ceremony to pay tribute to Confucius. The ceremony consists of four parts—music, other songs, dance, and ritual—each of which represents some aspect of the Confucian tradition. From this wonderful memorial ceremony honoring the legacy of Confucius, I always get a strong spiritual feeling.

Wang Yongzhi
Professor at Northwest University
Xi'an, China

eating of coarse rice and the drinking of water, the using of one's elbow for a pillow, joy is to be found. Wealth and rank attained through immoral means have as much to do with me as passing clouds" (*Analects* 7.16).

The disciples of Confucius described him as one who neglected his meals in a spell of work, forgot his worries when overcome by joy, and was so absorbed in the joy of the *Dao* that he was unaware that old age was coming on him.

Mencius remarked that he had no greater joy than to find on self-examination that he was true to himself. A man, he said, delights in three things: that his parents are alive and his brothers well, that he is not ashamed to face heaven or men, and that he has the most talented pupils.

The Negative Golden Rule

Confucius is also known for his doctrine of reciprocity (*shu*), or, as it has been called in the West, the negative golden rule: Don't do to others what you don't want done to yourself. Mencius put it positively: "Try your best to treat others as you would wish to be treated yourself, and you will find that this is the shortest way to benevolence" (*Mencius* VII A.4).

It seems that Confucius realized how difficult it is to put all this into practice. He never claimed to be a paragon of virtue. In fact he claimed the opposite. He had failed to cultivate virtue, he said, and refused to claim *jen* for himself. He confessed that he had not practiced what he preached and exclaimed at one point, "How dare I claim to be a sage or benevolent man?" In another *Analects* entry he lamented his moral inability in terms reminiscent of Paul's cry of desperation in Romans 7: "It is these things that cause me concern: failure to cultivate virtue; failure to go more deeply into what I have learned; inability, when I am told what is right, to move to where it is; and inability to reform myself when I have defects" (*Analects* 7.3).

Therefore he advised those pursuing *jen* to be modest and self-effacing, particularly when society is immoral. They should admit their mistakes and not be afraid of mending their ways, nor should they hide the fact that they don't know something. They should constantly examine themselves for faults and opportunities to improve. When others fail to appreciate them, they should worry less about what others think and more about their own moral defects: "It is not the failure of others to appreciate your abilities that should trouble you but your own lack of them." The small person seeks things from others, but the superior person realizes that the most enduring prize comes from one's own character.

More than a century after Confucius, Mencius summed up this teaching:

Women in Confucian Society

Confucian society is male-oriented. Women are to submit to their fathers, then their husbands, and, if they live with their sons after their husbands die, even to their sons. Only male ancestors are venerated.

Unfortunately, this has led to the belief among many that a woman's greatest duty is to produce a son and that her opinions are not important. This mind-set may also be linked to numerous abortions and infanticides that are performed when it is learned the baby is a girl.

If others do not respond to your love with love, look into your own benevolence; if others do not return your courtesy, look into your own respect. In other words, look into yourself whenever you fail to achieve your purpose. When you are correct in your person, the Empire will turn to you (*Mencius* IV A.4).

Perhaps because he realized he did not live up to his own ideals, Confucius advised his followers to be humble. He said they should not be ashamed to seek advice of those below them in rank. He proclaimed he had learned from every other person—the good points he copied and the bad he tried to correct in himself. Repeatedly the Chinese sage advised his pupils to be "eager to learn," which meant constantly examining themselves and studying the ways of the *Dao*. It also meant learning the Chinese traditions of history, literature, and the arts. This was the genesis of the Chinese emphasis on education.

Filial Piety and the Five Relationships

Confucius said the basis of *jen* (benevolence) is filial piety and fraternal love. The first refers to the care and honor a son owes his father. He will feed his parents and revere them, without complaint, and protect his father's honor. Even if his father steals a sheep, the son should not reveal the crime. Fraternal love is the love between brothers.

Filial piety is the most important of the "five relationships," which have been the cornerstones of Chinese social structure: the father is to love the son, and the son revere the father; the older brother is to be gentle to the younger brother, and the latter respectful; the husband is to be good to the wife, and the wife should listen; the older friend should be considerate to a younger friend, and the younger should be deferential; the ruler should be benevolent to his subjects, while subjects should be loyal.

Notice the importance of age in Confucian society. Two vice presidents from my college, of similar age, attended a formal dinner at a university in Korea, where the Confucian influence is also strong. There was much talking and apparent confusion among the Korean hosts before the dinner until finally one asked the two American guests how old they were. When it was discovered that one was a year older than the other, suddenly there were smiles all around, and their places at the table were set. The older vice president found himself seated at the head of the table.

A Christian Perspective

Confucius and Mencius believed that heaven imparts an original moral sense to each person. This may be analogous to Paul's divine law "written on [our] hearts" (Rom. 2:14–15). But while they (especially Confucius) acknowledge their own failure to live by this moral sense, they don't know much about the holiness of heaven and assume we can perfect ourselves by our own unaided efforts. They taught things that have contributed to the oppression of women and laid the foundation for a rigid social structure that can stifle freedom and love.

As Swiss theologian Hans Küng has observed, Jesus went beyond the Confucian restrictions of love to family and nation; the wise man of Galilee wanted to overcome flesh and blood—and gender, for that matter—distinctions. Historian Jeffrey Wattles writes in his book *The Golden Rule* that while Confucianists can think of benevolence to others only by comparing them to their own family, Jesus gave a theological reason for loving others. They should be loved because they too are children of our common heavenly Father. While Confucius taught that enemies are to receive not love but correction, Jesus told his disciples they were to love their enemies because this is how God treats his enemies. And perhaps most important, Confucius knew we are called to live up to grand moral ideals but he had little to say to those who seek forgiveness and redemption.

Two Kinds of Daoism

Daoism is that other part of the Chinese religious mix. You recall that we explored Buddhism in the last chapter, and we just finished an overview of Confucianism—an ethical system that is also religious. Now we come to the last of the three major components of traditional Chinese religion—Daoism.

Just as we saw that Hinduism and Buddhism contain radically different religions within the "ism," there are radically different kinds of Daoism. In fact the two basic groups—religious Daoism and philosophical Daoism—could hardly be more different. Religious Daoists believe in gods with saving power, sinful human nature, and redemption from guilt and sin by means of prayer, penance, alchemy, and other rituals of personal religion. They seek immortality. Philosophical Daoists, on the other hand, are atheists who do not believe in life after death. Like Theravadin Buddhists, they aim to penetrate surface appearances to get at the hidden reality that animates the cosmos. They call this the *Dao* (Chinese for "way"). The two forms of Daoism are not completely disconnected, however; seeds for religious Daoism can be found in the earliest Daoist text, the *Dao De Jing* (or *Tao Te Ching*, circa fourth century

BC). So let's take a look at philosophical Daoism first, since its bible is the *Dao De Jing*.

Philosophical Daoism

Philosophical Daoism was a reaction against Confucianism. Lao Zi (otherwise known as Lao Tzu, sixth century BC), the supposed founder and author of the *Dao De Jing*, felt Confucius' teachings were too conformist and moralistic.

You could say he was rebelling against the establishment. Those of us who came of age in the 1960s will see in this section the reason the *Dao De Jing* became a favorite text for hippies rebelling against the American "establishment."

Lao Zi stressed the individual rather than society. If Confucius taught duty, restraint, and society, Lao Zi prized freedom, release, and nature—the way to do is to be. The *Dao De Jing* is a reaction against striving for *jen*, for it advocates instead *wu-wei*, which is literally "not doing," thus not striving. Its unifying theme is to get our eyes off society's norms and back onto our feelings and the nonrational (which is not necessarily *ir*rational) side of life.

THE DAO DE JING

We really don't know many particulars about the *Dao De Jing*. We know its title means "the book of the way and its virtues." (Notice that Lao Zi used the same word that Confucius used—the *Dao* or the Way—but defined it differently.) We're not sure of the date (only that the book appeared between the sixth and fourth centuries BC) or the author (only that he was the "old master," which is what Lao Zi means), and that he wrote it as he "departed for the West," the land of the dead. Some scholars even think this book was the work of several minds.

It is well known that the book never defines the *Dao* (the Way). A preliminary reading shows that the book is full of irony. For example, it says the *Dao* cannot be named, yet the whole book tries to tell its reader what it is and is not.

Another irony that is repeated throughout is that strength comes from weakness. Water, it says, is soft and yielding (it can be pierced by a baby's hand) but also hard and inflexible (it can cut through rock). We Christians would agree—we say a crucified man saved the world through "defeat," and the powerful Roman Empire was conquered by an unarmed band of religious people.

A major theme in the *Dao De Jing* is "returning to the root by nonaction [*wu-wei*]." Another translation of *wu-wei* is "nonstriving." The idea is not inaction but naturalness and not overdoing—doing only what is necessary and natural. This is the picture of a person who "goes with the flow," which frees up her natural abilities to be used as they were meant to be, instead of being frustrated when things don't go her way. She withdraws from the customary pleasures and thinking of society to get to what Daoists call the roots of reality. The result, they say, is contentment and humility.

An example of this lifestyle would be refusing to retaliate against an enemy but rather watching him (and the *Dao* or nature) destroy himself. That's the nature of evil—it will eventually be reversed. The philosophical Daoist is confident that the cosmos has this ironic structure, even though she thinks there is no personal God who put it there.

Some have called philosophical Daoism a philosophy of camouflage because its underlying theme is that reality is not what it seems. Lao Zi says, "The greatest cleverness appears like stupidity; the greatest eloquence seems like stuttering." Think of Socrates who was considered politically and socially stupid by the rulers of Athens, and Jesus whose wisdom was dismissed by the Pharisees.

Lao Zi also said that virtue comes not from calculation but union. In other words, we become good not so much by gritting our teeth and flexing our muscles and will as by trying to float on the stream of the *Dao* and letting it carry us along. There is a similar concept in Christian faith, but the analogy is very imperfect because the *Dao* is impersonal, whereas the Christian God is supremely personal. But consider Mother Teresa. Most of the world thought her prime ministry was to the poor. She corrected reporters when they said this and always insisted her first ministry was to

Continued on page 79

Jesus. And more to our point, she asserted that he was the source of her strength and virtue. She said the only way she did what she did was to go to Mass each morning to receive strength and new life from the Son of God himself. Her virtue came through union with God, not simply through her own effort.

Lao Zi and his disciple Zhuang Zi (also known as Chuang Tzu) taught a kind of cosmic humility that realizes our own nothingness (in comparison with the totality of the cosmos) and becomes forgetful of ourselves "like a dry tree stump" or "dead ashes." Wise people "know themselves but do not see themselves." In other words, they are not obsessed with themselves and their own spiritual progress but recognize their nothingness before the *Dao*. (This is like Christian disciples who forget themselves and are in love with the One who mysteriously fills them and lives through them.) They have come to understand with Zhuang Zi that "you never find happiness until you stop looking for it." He found that when he stopped trying to be happy, suddenly "right" and "wrong" became apparent all by themselves. Happiness came also but only as a by-product of union with the *Dao*. Therefore people of the *Dao* are unconcerned with whether people like or dislike them, respect them or not. "For where there are many men, there are also many opinions and little agreement. There is nothing to be gained from the support of a lot of nitwits who are doomed to end up in a fight with each other." Hence they "imitate the fish that swims unconcerned, surrounded by a friendly element, and minding its own business."[1]

CHRISTIAN REFLECTION

Continued from page 77

and natural catastrophes, Lao Zi would come again and inaugurate the age of Great Peace. Troubles had come because of human sin. Therefore people should confess their sins and drink sanctified water. Then they would be immune to danger; if they died in battle, it would be because of insufficient faith or confession. Chinese people gave up their belongings, contributed to the poor, and built roads and bridges in this mass movement. Before long, government troops killed Chang, but the movement survived him.

Lao Zi and Zhuang Zi gave little hint of believing that the divine was anything more than an impersonal fate; they insisted nonetheless that its workings are good—if not for the individual at least for humanity overall. Resigning themselves to what is and cannot be changed was a way to throw themselves into the abyss of goodness and be content that all would be well.

> If we are delighted even to be in a human form alone, insofar as the human form changes in myriad ways, without ever an end, the enjoyment therein must be incalculable. Therefore sages will roam where nothing can get away and everything is there. For them, youth is good and so is old age; for them, the beginning is good and so is the end.
>
> Zhuang Zi
> *Chuang Tzu*, Inner Chapters, Chapter 6

The vast majority of the Lao Zi and Zhuang Zi texts speak of an abstract and impersonal *Dao*. But there are hints in Zhuang Zi that the reason that the whole system is good is that there is a beneficent Being ordering what is. He tells a story of Tzu Lai, a man on the brink of death who explains to his family, "What makes my life good is also what makes my death good. . . . Now if you consider the universe as a great forge and the creator as a great smith, what could happen that would not be all right? I go to sleep relaxed and perk up when I wake" (*Chuang Tzu*, Inner Chapters, chap. 6).

Nevertheless, there are of course huge discrepancies between this faith and Christian faith. First and foremost, for the philosophical Daoist this is a lonely and chilly universe, without a God of love who brings his people back to himself. We can get a peek of the chilliness from the story of Zhuang Zi, who sang and drummed on a bowl when his wife died. Asked for an explanation by a shocked friend, he replied, "This is like the rotation of the four seasons—spring, summer, fall, and winter. Now she lies asleep in the great house of the universe. For me to go about weeping and wailing would be to show my ignorance of destiny. Therefore I don't" (*Chuang Tzu* 18).

Second, there is a sense of fatalism and passivity that do not fit a world run by a God who seeks our participation in the establishment of his kingdom through our obedience and prayer.

Third, Daoists tend to believe that if we would just get rid of duty and formalized learning, people would naturally do right and good things, which they now resist doing. This seems hard to believe after the Holocaust, the killing fields of Cambodia, Stalin's Gulag, and the genocide in Darfur. This Daoist belief depends on, what Christians consider, a naive confidence in the goodness of human nature. The Christian doctrine of original sin (humans are predisposed to selfishness) seems more realistic. And that's exactly why Christians say we can't follow the Chinese Way or Christ's Way without a Savior to enable us.

Religious Daoism

The Scriptures tell us that everyone knows in some sense that there is a God (Rom. 1:19–21). Perhaps this is the reason there was a shift around the second century AD from philosophical Daoism, which is atheistic, to religious Daoism, which believes in all sorts of gods. Most people have a hard time living with atheism, or a moral universe that lacks a personal god. We are persons, and according to Paul's first chapter in Romans, we all have a latent or subconscious intuition that at the foundation of the cosmos is a Person not just an abstract principle. Thus it was perhaps inevitable that philosophical Daoism would produce another Daoism that made room for a god or gods.

It started with the desire of early Daoists for immortality. The earliest doctrine that human beings are merged with the *Dao*, thus losing their individuality, was not very attractive to some. They were inspired by Zhuang Zi's stories of "pure men of old" who climbed to great heights, could not be burned by fire or drowned in water, and lived on wonderful islands. Later Daoists, inspired by these visions, built a system devoted to gaining immortality.

They devised a variety of methods to avert death. Some used alchemy, ingesting mixtures

Daoist Priests

The Daoist priest is often a charismatic individual who knows the rituals for various festivals and can exorcise demons from buildings and people. He is something of a continuation of the ancient Chinese shaman, who was believed to be possessed by spirits and could communicate with them.

Mao Zedong and Religious Daoism

The founder of the modern Communist state in China, *Mao Zedong* (1893–1976), enforced official atheism but seems to have believed privately in a realm beyond the grave. In 1957 he wrote a poem addressed to Li, a woman who lost her husband Liu (which literally means "willow"). Mao's own wife was Yang (literally, "poplar"). The thoughts expressed are reminiscent of a religious Daoist cosmos.

> Long have I lost my Yang, the brave poplar tree
> And Liu, your spreading willow, is now cut down.
> But silken haired poplar seeds and willow wisps
> *Float up, as did they, to the ninth heaven.*
> Passing the moon, they tarried, and . . .
> Were given to drink of gold cassia wine.
> *And the goddess of the moon honored these*
> *Loyal souls, with her sleeves spread, dancing for them*
> *All through the boundless spaces of the sky.*[2]

of lead, mercury, and gold. This of course killed a good many! But later Daoists were motivated by the fourth-century story of a Wei Po-Yang, who gave the potion to his dog. The dog died immediately. Wei figured, however, that it might work only for human beings, and it would be better to risk death than miss out on what might be his only chance of immortality. Unfortunately, the potion also killed poor Wei. But when Wei's disciple found his body, the disciple imagined that Wei must have known something that he didn't. So he too ingested the stuff and the same thing happened to him. When two more disciples found these two dead men and a dead dog, they decided they would not make the same mistake and left to get some coffins. While they were gone, the story went, Wei and his disciple and the dog all came back to life, left a message behind, and proceeded into immortality.

Other Daoists tried elaborate breathing exercises, less toxic forms of alchemy, good deeds, special diets, and even certain sexual practices—all in the quest for immortality.

The efforts to gain immortality were set in the context of gods and cosmic forces. The usual view of the cosmos went like this: The supreme *Dao* is an unchanging and impersonal principle that is the origin of all things. It gave birth to a "breath" (*ch'i*) that in turn gave rise by movement to the active principle, *yang,* and by stillness to the principle of rest, *yin.* This world is the result of the continual interaction of yin and yang with the five fundamental agents of the world—wood, fire, earth, metal, and water. The winter months show the dominance of yin's inactivity—coldness, wetness, dormancy, darkness. The summer months show that yang's dynamism has won out, producing warmth, activity, and light.

Somehow the Dao has also produced a hierarchy of gods, with the three Heavenly Worthies at the top. These represent a sort of Daoist trinity, with the supreme deity as an emanation of the Dao, Lord Dao as the personification of the Dao, and Lord Lai who is Lao Zi turned into a god. Below this trinity is a vast bureaucracy of gods who inhabit nine different heavens, and after that are enormous numbers of demons, humans, animals, and ghosts.

Religious Daoism presents an interesting spectacle for the Christian. It recognizes rightly that there is more to supernatural reality than the impersonal *Dao* and that we are sinners who have a chance of attaining life after death. But attaining this life is all up to us and our feeble efforts, using methods that appear to be hopeless, and we don't receive much help from the gods. This is where a real God who truly entered history to deal with sin once and for all, and who is able to promise eternal life, is far more attractive.

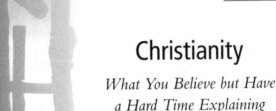

Christianity

*What You Believe but Have
a Hard Time Explaining*

Jesus is the center and heart of Christianity.
Apart from Jesus there is no Christianity. If
Christianity is ever explained in a way that does
not put Jesus at the center, it isn't Christian any
longer. Trying to explain Christianity in this
way may seem hard to imagine, but there have
been many people who have done just that,
knowingly and unknowingly. For example,
there have always been those who have said
Christianity is a way of life more than anything
else, and this way of life is having faith in God
while loving our neighbors. That may be a nice
way to live, but it isn't Christianity. You can call
it Unitarianism or theism or religious humanism (or even Judaism or Islam!), but you really

shouldn't call it Christianity. It's possible, of course, to have faith in God and love your neighbors and deny the very essence of Christian doctrine, which is that Jesus is God come to earth to save sinful humanity.

So in this chapter on Christianity we will start with Jesus. And to find him, we will go to the book of Mark, the shortest and perhaps the earliest Gospel in the Bible. We go to a New Testament Gospel because, as Martin Luther once said, we have no sure knowledge of Jesus except through the Bible. Our only reliable knowledge of Jesus comes from these Gospels that were written by those close to him and assembled by those who were devoted to what the apostles taught.

Jesus, according to Mark

The central question of Mark's Gospel is "But who do you say that I am?" (8:29). This was the question Jesus asked his followers when they were sitting together one day, and it is also the key question that gets to the essence of Christianity: Who is Jesus?

Mark tells us at the very beginning of his Gospel that Jesus is the "Son of God" (1:1). Then at the end we hear it again in the mouth of the centurion: "Surely this man was the Son of God!" (15:39 NIV). Mark is telling us that only when we face the crucifixion and learn its meaning can we know Jesus for who he is—the Son of God.

While reading the first half of Mark's Gospel, we might expect a different end to the story. Jesus seems to be a miracle worker or magician—healing the sick, raising the dead, casting out demons, and walking on water. And his disciples are unaware of what he is up to. They don't understand his parables (4:13; 7:17–18), are afraid and have no faith (4:40), and fail to comprehend the multiplication of the loaves that fed five thousand people (6:52). In chapter 8 they have forgotten all about that miraculous feeding, because this time they ask Jesus, "How can one feed these people with bread here in the desert?" (v. 4).

Mark includes these details to tell us, among other things, that miracles don't convey meaning by themselves. In other words, people can see miracles without understanding the miracle worker. Eventually the disciples came to see that Jesus is the long-expected Messiah. But even then they followed the trend of their day, which was to think the Messiah would be a political and military leader who would throw out the Romans. They failed to understand what Jesus tried to explain repeatedly, that the Messiah would have to die.

After Peter confesses that Jesus is the Messiah at Caesarea Philippi (8:29), and Jesus begins his lonely journey to what awaits him in Jerusalem, the miracles nearly cease (there are only one exorcism, one healing, and the withering of the fig tree). The Gospel concentrates instead on explaining the cross, through which Jesus gives his life as a "ransom for many" (10:45); the blood that Jesus sheds on the cross is the blood of a new covenant (agreement between God and his people), which is "poured out for many" (14:24). Jesus was clearly echoing Isaiah's description of the suffering servant who

Today some people think the New Testament canon (the collection of twenty-seven books under that name) was decided by a small group of males and imposed on a movement that had actually accepted a larger and more diverse collection of books.

But the facts are quite different. In selecting the books for the New Testament canon, the leaders of the church merely ratified what the churches had already determined at the grass roots. They said, in effect, "These are the books that have been recognized as authoritative by nearly all the churches." They used three criteria: apostolic (were they written by apostles or their followers?), conformity to the rule of faith (are they congruent with what the apostles taught?), and acceptance by the church at large (were these books accepted by nearly all the churches?).

Books were rejected when they failed to meet these criteria. For example, the Gospel of Thomas teaches things foreign to what the apostles said Jesus taught. It has Jesus saying, "Lift up a stone, and you'll find me there," and "Let Mary go away from us, because women are not worthy of life."

Some books, such as James, Hebrews, and Revelation were accepted more slowly than others. Professor Bruce Metzger, expert on the history of the canon, says this shows that the early church was careful to take time to determine whether a document was authentic.

> ### Christianity
>
> 1. Ultimate concern: union with the triune God, while retaining individuality
> 2. View of reality:
>   a. God: holy, just, loving; triune (Father, Son, and Holy Spirit); infinite yet personal
>   b. Self: created good but fallen, in bondage to sin (apart from redemption)
>   c. World: good, finite, a creation of a good God
> 3. Basic human problem: sin, which separates from God
> 4. Resolution: Christ, whose perfect life merits our salvation and whose death pays the penalty for our sin; we are joined to Christ by faith, which is the beginning of the new birth and filling by the Holy Spirit.

would make an "offering for sin" and would bear the sins of many (53:10–11).

In other words, in the cross God was dealing with the sins of his people. These sins had broken fellowship between the holy God and a sinful people. Christian theologians have used more than several theories to explain how this "atonement" works. No one theory is sufficient, probably all are necessary, and still we don't fully understand. But the New Testament makes clear, building on strong themes in the Old Testament, that God could bring a sinful people to himself only by the blood of the cross.

Jews and Muslims, among others, ask why God couldn't have forgiven us without the cross. Jesus said repeatedly that he "must" go to the cross (see, for example, Mark 8:31–32). This was based on the Jewish conviction that sins must be atoned for (literally, "covered") by blood and the human (God-given!) intuition that, for justice to be done, evil must be punished. Therefore God cannot ignore evil when he forgives sin, lest evil be condoned and his holiness be compromised.

Blood is necessary because in the Bible and all ancient cultures blood represents life. Evil destroys life, and justice demands that another life be given to compensate for the one taken. Most world religions have practiced animal sacrifice for this reason.

On the cross of Christ, love and justice are simultaneously displayed: justice because here God punished evil, and love because God took the punishment on himself. The early church said the cross is at the heart of the gospel (literally, "good news"), for there, because of his holy love, God saved rebellious human beings by taking on himself the punishment and abandonment ("My God, my God, why have you abandoned me?" Matt. 27:46, my translation), which human sin deserves.

Mark's Gospel shows us why we need the cross. Jesus tries to teach humility to the disciples, but they don't get it. Instead, they argue about who will be the greatest and who will get to sit on his right and left hands when his kingdom comes (Mark 9:33–34; 10:35–37). Then at the time of trial, when Jesus asks for their help, they all fall away—even his closest followers. Some, in an ironic twist, take a nap (14:32–38). Peter blusters about following Jesus to the death but

Catholics and Protestants: How Are They Different?

The most basic difference between Catholics and Protestants is that Protestants regard God as coming to the believer through the Word preached and read, and Catholics say God comes typically through the "mediation" of the church. The five points below flow from this basic difference.

1. *Authority*. Catholics say their final appeal for truth and morals is the *magisterium* or collection of Roman Catholic traditions. Protestants appeal to the Bible. Protestants claim they are looking to God's Word rather than human words, but Catholics say the Holy Spirit has inspired the magisterium to interpret the Bible properly.
2. *Salvation*. In their official theologies both Catholics and Protestants say salvation is the work of Jesus Christ, not our own works, that saves us and that we receive the benefit of this work by faith, which is active in love. Catholics tend to stress the works of love, and Protestants emphasize faith.
3. *Ministry*. Catholics say the grace of Christ is received particularly through the seven sacraments administered by male priests, who receive an indelible mark when they are ordained. Most Protestant denominations ordain women as well as men and do not believe in the indelible mark on the ordained.
4. *Worship*. The Catholic Mass has a sermon, which is typically short, and leads to the culmination of worship in the Eucharist (communion). Most Protestants believe the preached Word is the climax of the service, so their sermons are usually longer.

Continued on page 91

Christianity • 89

I wake in the middle of the night and lie listening. From far away the drums reach my ears. Someone is dying. Someone is suffering. Someone already died. It's almost dawn and the drums invoke the demons that they are trying to summon. Lying in bed, I ask for God's mercy and protection.

From far away as I lie in bed, I hear other drums. These are coming from a church. It's Sunday morning and, although I cannot distinguish the words, I know they are praising Jesus.

The drums they use to invoke demons make a sound like a groan of pain and disillusion. To praise Jesus they also beat drums, but their sound soars with joy and gratitude. The voices begin to rise high and fine. Tears of emotion descend from the eyes and for a few moments it feels like we could be in the kingdom itself. This is the way we praise the Lord in Africa.

As I join this worship, I think about Jesus Christ, how good he is, how he so deserves my praise. I sing of his love, his justice, and how much I love his name.

Later during the week, when I am alone, my lips may not be moving and no sound may be escaping from my mouth, but I am singing in my heart. I sing strong and high. I sing of Jesus' return, of my desire to be with him, and of my gratitude for all he has done for me. Whether in the silence of my room, behind the wheel of my car, or in the middle of the night when I awake, I sing of his faithfulness and mercy.

Noemia Gabriel Cessito
Nurse and Director of Project Life Medical Clinic
Dondo, Mozambique

eventually denies him three times. Afterward, he weeps in despair.

In the disciples we see ourselves—the weakness of our own flesh, the deceitfulness of our own hearts, and the darkness of our own minds when we face temptation. We realize that it is precisely because we are so frequently unfaithful—which we know if we listen keenly to the demands of God's law in the Bible and in our own conscience—that we need the cross. We know that our unholiness can never stand in the presence of the infinitely holy God and that only an infinite sacrifice can deal with our sin.

In Mark's Gospel Jesus calls his disciples to suffering discipleship. There is not a hint of watering down the lofty requirements of God's law. We are not told it will be easy. In fact Jesus tells us to take up our own cross on a daily basis (8:34).

Jesus calls us to love God and neighbor (12:29–31), but in Mark's Gospel that love is made of stern stuff. It isn't just a warm feeling but rather the way of obedience to the will of God, entailing repentance (1:15), self-denial (8:34), humility (9:35), giving to the poor and God's work (10:21), service (10:43–45), prayer and forgiveness (11:25), and persecution (10:30; 13:13). We are to obey even if that means cutting off a foot or gouging out an eye (9:43–47). Being Jesus' disciple means following his way regardless of the cost.

Continued from page 89

5. *Miscellaneous.*

a. *Apocrypha.* These are books such as Tobit, 1 and 2 Maccabees, and Wisdom, which are in Catholic but not Protestant Bibles. Generally the Church Fathers regarded them as inspired, but Luther and Calvin rejected them because most Jews in Israel at the time of Jesus did not put them in the Old Testament canon, and Catholics used them to support some debated doctrines such as purgatory.

b. *Mary and the saints.* Catholics pray to Mary and the saints, asking them to intercede for them before the Trinity, but Protestants don't. Catholics say it is like asking another Christian on earth to intercede; Protestants say there is no biblical precedent for it.

c. *Purgatory.* Catholics believe purgatory is a place or state in which the sins of those on the way to heaven are "purged" before meeting the holy God. Protestants do not find this in the Bible.

Another telling mark of this Gospel is the insider-outsider theme. God seems to love to do reversals. It is those on the outside of society—the low and despised, such as lepers, prostitutes, children, and the blind—who receive the Good News gladly. Those who have prestige in society—both religious and political leaders and some of the wealthy—are the ones who most typically reject it.

Like the other three, Mark's Gospel ends with the resurrection of Jesus from the dead. We aren't told there exactly what the resurrection means, but it is clearly a reason for great joy. The women at the tomb are told to go tell the apostles (16:7), and they in turn are commanded to tell the whole world (v. 15).

As a Christian who was baptized as a Catholic, to worship Jesus Christ and follow his example are inseparably integral parts of my life. Every day I read the Bible, especially the two readings and Gospel for Sunday Mass. Using the Vatican II Sunday Missal, and kneeling in front of a crucifix and picture of the holy family, I reflect on what Jesus Christ did to save us sinful human beings and how he teaches us to follow him.

Every Sunday I go to church and enjoy Mass with all my fellow brothers and sisters there. From 9 to 9:20 we sing the hymns with the accompaniment of a sister's piano playing, from 9:20 to 9:30 we say the rosary in the same rhythm, and from 9:30 to 10:30 or so we have Mass. The Holy Week before Easter always means a lot to me, especially the triduum (from holy Thursday through Easter Sunday). I am moved almost to tears by the bishop's washing the feet of twelve chosen brothers in the holy Thursday Mass, our touching the cross one by one in the holy Friday Mass, and then our lighting candles for each other in the dark during Mass on holy Saturday. On these occasions, I see as if in visions the living Lord among us. In this paschal mystery, I feel I am reborn into Jesus' death and resurrection.

It is not enough to worship our Lord in private and public without bearing our cross daily in the footsteps of Jesus. And to help and love those in need is a worship that will bring its own miracle.

Shang Quanyu
Professor of historical philosophy
Zhanjiang Normal University, China

The First Theologian

We are given more of the meaning of Jesus, and his death and resurrection, by the church's first theologian, the apostle Paul. You could call his letter to the Romans the early church's first systematic presentation of the gospel.

Paul begins by telling us that God has every right to be angry with us, for he has given us unmistakable evidence of his existence and care, but we have suppressed this knowledge, refused to give him the thanks and submission he deserves (Rom. 1:21), and turned to worship the gods of self and desire (vv. 22–32). God is easily seen in nature (vv. 19–20), and his law can be heard in our conscience (2:14–15), so we are without excuse. Even the religious are condemned because they do the very things for which they condemn the unreligious (vv. 17–29).

The result is that all human beings have turned in on themselves and away from their Creator. Because God's law prescribes perfect love for God and neighbor, and we have done just the opposite, all of us must keep silence before God. None of us will be justified in his sight by what we do (3:19–20). No amount of good deeds can compensate for our disobedience and idolatry. All that we can see, when we look carefully at God's law, is that we have broken it time and again, and we seem in fact to be lawbreakers by nature (v. 20).

The solution to our problem is not something we do but what Jesus Messiah (the Hebrew equivalent of "Christ") has done in his perfect life, death, and resurrection. His death on the cross was a sacrifice of atonement for our sins (v. 25), his life of perfect obedience earned the moral goodness the Law requires of us (5:19), and his resurrection brings us into union with our holy Father by joining us to the holy Son (6:5; 8:9–11).

In Romans we see the raw material for what the later church called mystical union with Christ. This is the idea that we are joined to Messiah Jesus not just symbolically but as truly as a branch is joined to the trunk of a tree. So when Jesus died on the cross, we died. And when Jesus rose from the dead, we rose with him. We are really with him now in his heavenly places, Paul tells us elsewhere (Eph. 2:6; Col. 3:1), even while we struggle on earth. But when the general resurrection takes place after the final judgment, we will be joined with him in body where we are now only in spirit.

In the eighth chapter of Romans Paul introduces us to the Holy Spirit, the Third Person in what Christians call the Trinity—the mysterious way in which God is at the same time three persons (Father, Son, and Holy Spirit). Paul tells us that the Christian life is life *in* the Spirit. In other words, we are joined to Jesus and we are to follow Jesus, but both of these things take place by the Spirit. We are joined to Jesus by the Spirit, and we follow Jesus only by the power of the Spirit. This is why the Christian life cannot be understood apart from the Spirit. A person is a Christian only if he has the Spirit (v. 9); by the Spirit we are set free from the law of sin and death (v. 2); the Spirit gives us life and peace (v. 6); the Spirit will raise our bodies from the dead (v. 11); by the Spirit we put to death the misdeeds of the flesh (v. 13); the Spirit makes us children of God, and we cry "Abba!" ("Daddy") (vv. 15–16); the Spirit helps us pray in our weakness (v. 26); the Spirit intercedes for us according to the will of God (v. 27).

In chapter 12 Paul describes the ethical life of the Christian. She is not conformed to the ways of the world but transformed by the renewing of her mind (v. 2); does not think of herself too highly (v. 3); practices love and hatred of evil (v. 9), generosity and hospitality (v. 13), and nonretaliation (vv. 14, 17, 19–20); and tries to live at peace with other people, insofar as that is possible without compromising her faith (v. 18).

In chapters 14 and 15 Paul tells believers how to get along with one another. They should not quarrel over minor matters but agree to disagree when it does not involve core issues of faith. And most important, they should not judge the hearts of others who disagree with them (14:10, 13).

This and other sections show Paul's concern for the church. He regarded it as indispensable to Christian faith. In fact he said that the church is "the body of Christ" (1 Cor. 12:27), and he said this in a letter addressed to a dysfunctional church! In other words, when we are in a local body of believers, we are actually connected to the life of Christ himself. The other side of this is disturbing—if we stop participating in church, we are cutting ourselves off from the life of Christ. This is a hard saying, but it is important in this age when it is fashionable to say, "I am spiritual but don't like organized religion." Jesus organized his followers and made clear provisions for later disciples to continue this organization (Matt. 16:18).

The Spread of Christianity

One might think that a new religion, whose founder was executed in a humiliating and barbarous fashion (Jesus was probably stripped naked before being nailed to the cross) and who exhorted his followers to be prepared for the same, would not do very well. But quite the opposite took place. The little movement, whose members were persecuted from its very first days, grew by leaps and bounds. After starting out tiny and fearful of the mighty Roman Empire, and comprised mainly of the poor and disenfranchised, it eventually conquered this same empire in less than three centuries.

Historian Kenneth Scott Latourette once listed a number of reasons for this unprecedented historical turnaround:

1. *Burning conviction* that beat the competition. These early believers knew their God (of course the only God) had come to earth into real history to save humanity. They also knew that he rose from the dead, thus confirming that what had happened on the cross was not a tragedy but a victory. There was nothing in the Greek and Roman religions, including their mystery religions, that came close to having a real god come into real history.
2. *Power* for a moral life. The Stoics also taught a moral life that attracted many. But there was no inner power attached to that religion. Only the Christian church could say they had the Spirit from God who enabled them to live an exemplary moral life.
3. The visible *courage and joy of the martyrs*. Millions of people in the empire saw and heard the selfless devotion of thousands of Christians who endured suffering and death rather than compromise their faith. Their public example inspired thousands more.

4. *Intellectual coherence* of the faith. Early Christian theology answered the most basic questions of life with coherence and sophistication. In the second century, for example, Justin Martyr had been devoted to Greek philosophy but then found that the Logos (the Stoic word for the organizing principle of the cosmos) had taken historical shape in Jesus of Nazareth. The great Augustine was impressed by the incarnation and humility of Jesus, neither of which he had found in Neoplatonism.

5. *Fellowship and friendship* in the midst of a giant, impersonal empire. Christian churches, despite their divisions, were the most inclusive and strongest associations in the empire. They cared for their poor, the imprisoned, and the elderly and infirm. In times of distress they shared food and money. Believers could find friends no matter what city they visited. Only the Jews had such an international network of fellowship, but theirs was racial. The Christian church appealed to men and women from all races and classes. It provided meaning for both the simple and the learned. Membership in the pagan mystery religions was often expensive, but the church was free, and most members were poor.

The Da Vinci Code

The megaseller *The Da Vinci Code* suggests that the true but suppressed Christianity was actually goddess worship found in such works as the Gospel of Philip and the Gospel of Mary; that the male, woman-hating church leaders eliminated the divine feminine from their Gospels; and that Jesus was not God in the New Testament but was made divine by Emperor Constantine in the fourth century.

This makes for a breathless tale but it doesn't have a historical leg to stand on. First of all, Gnosticism (see sidebar on p. 93) and its celebration of the divine feminine didn't arise until the second century, after the New Testament books were already written. Second, Jesus was considered divine from the very beginning, as the Gospels show. For example, when Jesus says to the paralytic, "Your sins are forgiven" (Mark 2:5), the Jews were outraged, calling it blasphemy and saying, "Who can forgive sins but God alone?" (v. 7). So Jesus was claiming divinity at the beginning of his ministry in this, the earliest Gospel.

6. *High moral standards.* All other religions but Judaism permitted their devotees to participate in cults that often included immoral celebrations of drunkenness and sexual debauchery. Infanticide and abortion were also widespread. Christians condemned all these things. They held up standards that seemed beyond human reach, but at the same time promised a power to grow toward them.

7. *The promise of immortality.* Most Greco-Roman religions promised immortality only for the superstars of the state or, in the case of the mystery religions, for those who could afford their rites. But the Christian church offered the promise of resurrection for every believer, rich or poor, elite or plebeian.[1]

Protestants vs. Roman Catholics

In this last part of the chapter, I'll answer some questions my students typically ask. The first is what separates Roman Catholics and Protestants. First I tell them the most basic distinction is that Protestants regard God as coming to the believer through the Word preached and read, and Catholics say God typically comes through the "mediation" of the church. Several differences flow from that basic distinction:

1. *Authority.* Catholics say their final appeal for truth and morals is the *magisterium,* or collection of Roman Catholic traditions. Protestants appeal to the Bible. Protestants claim they are looking to God's Word rather than human words, but Catholics say the Holy Spirit has inspired the *magisterium* to interpret the Bible properly.

2. *Salvation.* In their official theologies both Catholics and Protestants say it is the work of Jesus Christ, not our own

works, that saves us, and that we receive the benefit of this work by faith that is active in love. Catholics tend to stress the works of love, and Protestants emphasize the faith itself.

3. *Ministry*. Catholics say the grace of Christ is received particularly through the seven sacraments administered by male priests, who receive an indelible mark when they are ordained. Most Protestant denominations ordain women but do not believe in the indelible mark on the ordinand.

4. *Worship*. The Catholic mass has a sermon, which is typically short and leads to its culmination in the Eucharist (communion). Protestants typically believe the preached Word is the climax of the service, so their sermons are usually longer.

5. *Apocrypha*. These are books such as Tobit, 1 & 2 Maccabees, and Wisdom, which are in Catholic but not Protestant Bibles. The Fathers generally regarded them as inspired, but Luther and Calvin rejected them because most Jews in Israel at the time of Jesus did not put them in the Old Testament canon, and Catholics used them to support some debated doctrines such as purgatory.

6. *Mary and the saints*. Catholics pray to Mary and the saints, asking them to intercede for them before the Trinity, but Protestants don't. Catholics say it is like asking another Christian on earth to intercede; Protestants say there is no biblical precedent for it.

7. *Purgatory*. Catholics believe this is a place or state in which the sins of those on the way to heaven are purged before meeting the all-holy God. Protestants do not find it in the Bible.

Protestant Denominations

Martin Luther (1483–1546) started the Protestant Reformation and the group that later took his name—*Lutherans*. He and his followers hold to three *solas*: *sola gratia* (grace alone), *sola scriptura* (Scripture alone), and *sola fidei* (faith alone). That is, they hold that humans are saved by grace, which means a free gift (Christ's work on the cross for them); they believe that our final authority is the Bible alone and not human tradition or reason not submitted to revelation; and they affirm that we receive that gift not because of our good works but through faith. Lutherans rejected Catholic transubstantiation (the bread and wine at communion change their substance to the body and blood of Christ), but believe in a Real Presence in which the real body and blood of Christ are "in, with, and under" the bread and wine.

Episcopalians are the American branch of the worldwide *Anglican* communion, started by the Church of England, which in the sixteenth century followed Luther away from Rome. The Anglicans kept the essentials of Catholic worship but added Luther's doctrine of justification (salvation by faith) and emphasis on preaching, and Calvin's doctrine of sanctification (the process of becoming holy). Their *Book of Common Prayer* is widely regarded as the most beautiful literary form of worship in the English language.

Presbyterians are descended from the Reformed branch of the sixteenth-century Reformation, especially the work of John Calvin (1509–1564) and Huldrych Zwingli (1484–1531). Calvin said the churches of an area should be led by a group of elders with the ministers, collectively known as a "presbytery," hence the name. The Reformed also believe in a Real Presence in communion but in a more "spiritual" sense. They place great emphasis on sanctification.

Baptists are descended from the Anabaptists of the sixteenth century, who said faith requires a decision. Therefore Christians who were baptized as infants need to be baptized again (*ana* in Greek) and by immersion after they decide for Christ. American Baptists were influenced by the seventeenth-century English Baptists who believed in just war, unlike the German Anabaptists who were pacifists,. Today's *Mennonites* and *Amish* are descended from the sixteenth-century Anabaptists. All of these groups believe the local congregation (not a national body) should govern itself; they also reject a prescribed liturgy.

Methodists stem from the English Awakening of the eighteenth century led by John Wesley (1703–1791). Wesley was a priest in the Church of England, who was forced out of the church and into the open fields to preach the need to be born again, because the established church would not let him do so. Wesley taught justification by faith along with the pursuit of holiness, while valuing liturgy and the Eucharist.

The differences noted in these denominations are not as great as the more profound divide that runs through every one of these denominations, between what are often called the "progressives" and the "orthodox." The former tend to use modern experience and social science to judge what they can accept from the Bible, while the latter point to the biblical vision and the history of the theological tradition as their touchstones. This difference in focus leads to differing conclusions about sexuality (at the forefront of debate today), whether Jesus is the only way to God, and whether the New Testament's portrait of Jesus and the apostles provides the final standard for truth and morality.

Evangelicals versus Fundamentalists

This last distinction is the most misunderstood today. Most people think evangelical Christians and fundamentalist Christians are the same, but there are some important differences.

Fundamentalists tend to read the Bible more literally, while evangelicals tend to look more carefully at genre and literary and historical context. Fundamentalists question the value of human culture that is not created by Christians or related to the Bible, whereas evangelicals see God's "common grace" working in and through all human culture. Fundamentalists tend to restrict their social witness to protests against homosexual practice and abortion, but evangelicals also want to fight racism, sexism, and poverty. Often fundamentalists want to separate themselves from liberal Christians (which to them sometimes means evangelicals), while evangelicals are more willing to work with other Christians toward common religious and social goals.

While both groups preach salvation by grace, fundamentalists tend to focus so much on rules and restrictions (dos and don'ts) that their hearers can get the impression that Christianity means following behavioral rules. Evangelicals, on the other hand, focus more on the person and work of Christ and personal relationship with him, as the heart of Christian faith.

Shinto

The National Religion of Japan

Let's start our exploration of the national religion of Japan by defining two important words—*Shinto* and *Japan*.

Shinto means "the way of the gods." The gods (called *kami*) are deities of sky and soil, nation and localities.

Japanese people revere their *kami* but not in the way that Christians worship Jesus. There is very little by way of a personal relationship. The *kami* are regarded as much more distant, and so devotion to them is reserved and formal.

The word *Japan* means "origin of the sun" or "land of the rising sun." This idea that the Japanese people are connected to the sun goes back to the myth at the center of Shinto.

The Myth of the Sun Goddess

The Japanese story of national origins is the myth of the Sun Goddess. Our earliest record of this goes back to AD 720. The world is said to have started in primordial chaos, out of which arose a succession of seven generations of gods. The seventh are brother and sister gods named Izanagi (the brother) and Izanami (the sister), who become husband and wife. Her urine, feces, and vomit become matter, earth, and ocean. They create the gods (*kami*) of nature (we might better call them "spirits"), and then three chief gods: Amaterasu Omikami, the Sun Goddess; the Moon God; and Susanowo, the god of storms and seas.

Pretty soon there's a fight between husband (Izanagi) and wife (Izanami), and Izanami dies as a result. But she's still alive in one sense, since she descends to the land of death and darkness, where she is covered with maggots. Izanagi follows her in grief, but when she pleads with him not to look at her shameful condition, he ignores her plea and says he will divorce her (it is not clear how she can be dead and divorced at the same time). In retaliation she declares she will kill one thousand of the human beings who belong to him (humans were created along with the *kami* and so are not entirely different). But he shouts in anger, "If you do that, I will create fifteen hundred new ones every day!" When he leaves the lower world, he washes off the impure demons that have grabbed onto him. Historians say this explains the Japanese obsession with purity and their belief in demons.

The Sun Goddess and her brother Susanowo then become the rulers of this world. She is the source of all life-giving power, food, agriculture, life, and order. He is rebellious, wild, and arrogant, and so causes much of the trouble we see around us. When he destroyed the Sun Goddess's rice fields and polluted her festival, she hid in a cave—which plunged the world into darkness. Only when the *kami* produced a mirror and jewels (the sacred objects of Shinto) was she persuaded to come out. She negotiated with her brother, and they agreed she would retain control over this world, and he over the mysterious worlds of magic, demons, and astrology.

It's important to note that the story suggests Susanowo (the Sun Goddess's brother) did not *intend* evil but did what he did because he didn't know any better and simply made some mistakes. This is why Shinto sees evil not as malevolent acts of the will but the unintended results of ignorance and error.

The Sun Goddess's grandson was Ninigi, who one day descended to earth to take power in Japan. He was given a sword as well as the mirror and jewels that were used to lure his grandmother from her cave. *His* great-grandson is said to have been Jimmu, the first human emperor of Japan. Shinto historians say Jimmu began his dynasty in 660 BC, and this was the origin of the current Japanese ruling family, which can be traced back to AD 720. In fact, this is the longest-lasting ruling dynasty in the world.

The Sun Goddess as Center

The myth of the Sun Goddess is what ties together most of Japanese religion—including folk religion and even Buddhism. Japanese folk religion revolves around agriculture and nature, both of which are said to depend on the blessing of the Sun Goddess.

There is an altar (*kamidana*) in the prayer room of my house. Inside the altar there is a wooden good luck charm called *ofuda*, wrapped in Japanese paper. This ensures that the *kami* stays within this sacred place. In front of it there are small plates filled with water, rice, and salt, and also the leaves of the sakaki tree.

Each morning the rice and water are changed and I pray at the altar by bowing twice, clapping my hands twice, and bowing once again. I always pray that my family will have a good and safe day.

On January 1 my whole family gathers in front of the altar and prays one by one for a safe and healthy year. There is a special table below the altar where we put ginkgo nuts, dried persimmon and chestnuts, dried squid, and a tangerine. Also we drink sake (rice wine) mixed with a special Chinese herb. We believe this will help us live a long and healthy life.

Atsushi Kakita
High school Japanese history teacher and Shinto priest
Osaka, Japan

The twice-a-year Nakatomi purification ritual, the annual Harvest Prayer Festival, and the annual Festival of First Fruits are all dedicated to the Sun Goddess.

You can see the Sun Goddess's connection to Buddhism when Shinto devotees say she is a manifestation of a Buddha. Yoshida Kanetomo, a fifteenth-century Shinto scholar, impressed on his readers and followers the idea that all Buddhist deities (bodhisattvas) are manifestations of *kami*. Since the Sun Goddess is in control of this world, and this world is filled with millions of *kami*, the Sun Goddess is superior to all Buddhist gods.

Shinto as State Religion

In the Meiji Restoration (1868–1912), when Japan opened itself to the West, she changed not only politically but also religiously. And the one was necessary to the other. Politically, the nation changed from a dictatorship to a Western-style republic under the emperor. Religiously, Japan rejected Buddhism (at least formally) and endorsed Shinto as its state religion. The Japanese people were required to enroll at Shinto shrines, and Buddhists were persecuted. Most Buddhist priests in fact shifted their allegiance overnight to Shinto, which had been made easier by the fifteenth-century scholar described above.

> ### Shinto Shamans
>
> A shaman is someone who communicates with the spirit world. Shinto shamans or *miko*, typically women, fall into a trance when they are thought to be possessed by a *kami*. Shamanistic rituals are performed when individuals ask for them—usually to choose a marriage partner or to determine the success of a business or farming endeavor. Some of the séances are used to find out the reason someone has come down with a disease or experienced some other bad turn. Typically the answer is that the person has offended a *kami* by neglect or action or failed to participate properly in a ritual.

The formal establishment of Shinto as *the* Japanese religion proceeded in three stages:

1. In 1870 the government announced that the *kami* had founded the nation, and state and religion were therefore united.
2. After foreigners and Buddhists protested, a Department of Religion was established for both "foreign religions" and for Buddhism. This became the Bureau of Shrines and Temples. In 1872 the practice of Christianity was officially permitted.
3. The Japanese government established state Shinto in 1882, and announced it was nonreligious. The idea was that Shinto was from the divine realm directly, while all other religions were made up by men. In this sense "religion" became the word for man-made philosophies.

The result of this process was a heightened role for Shinto in the minds of most Japanese. It also meant a strengthened nationalism. School textbooks taught the divine origin of the emperor's family and the uniquely divine character of the Japanese people.

Shinto and World War II

Was Pearl Harbor the result of this gradual elevation of Shinto into the religious mantle for the nation? Not quite.

As is often the case, political leaders used religion for their own purposes. This was not the first time that religion was used to build patriotism in Japan, but before this it wasn't Shinto. In the Nara period (eighth century AD) it was Buddhism, and in the Tokugawa period (seventeenth and eighteenth centuries) it was neo-Confucianism. So it was not Shinto that drove Japan to aggressive militarism in World War II but a political-military elite that exploited Shinto for its own purposes.

After the end of the war, the emperor declared, under pressure from the Americans, that he was just a man and not divine. Many knew this already of course, but some Shinto devotees were stunned. Shinto was no longer called nonreligious but a religion in actuality.

Today Japanese are less religious than they were before the war, perhaps because of Shinto's association with Japan's devastating defeat. Most Japanese are indifferent to the emperor politically, but they respect him at the very least as the foremost representative of the world's oldest ruling dynasty. More important, many take seriously the emperor's coronation with the Shinto *Daijosai* rite, the sacred ritual in which he is thought to be transformed from an ordinary mortal into the embodiment of the soul of Japan. He becomes, in other words, a *kami*. One indication of the continuing reverence paid to the emperor was the 1990 shooting of the mayor of Nagasaki after he said the emperor must accept some responsibility for the war.

Harmony with Nature

Shinto is what I would call a minimalist religion. It has little or no philosophy, and there is not much of a Shinto morality to speak of. It is concerned instead with being in harmony with nature.

After World War II, when Shinto was stigmatized by the nation's defeat and Buddhism was thought by many to be too complex for busy working people, new religions arose that promised Japanese answers to Japanese questions. Typically they promised that life's problems could be solved through faith and worship. Some practiced faith healing. Others guaranteed solutions to marital and financial problems. Some pledged financial prosperity.

The "New Religions" have several characteristics:

1. They often combine elements from other religions, saying they use the "best" from Buddhism, Shinto, and even Christianity.
2. A living person usually serves as either organizer or founder. This leader is considered divine or semidivine. His or her teachings become revealed scripture.
3. While previous Japanese religion tended to assume you were a member if you grew up in Japan, these religions ask individuals to make a personal faith commitment.

There is the sense in Shinto that the cosmos is disordered and must be brought into order. This is done by participation in Shinto ritual. Just as the Sun Goddess brought order to this world by her descendant, the emperor, devotees are to help bring order by their joining Shinto rites and ceremonies. This requires communing and communicating with the *kami*, and this takes place typically at a Shinto shrine.

The shrine is a sacred place, marked by wooden gates (*torii*), that is the special residence of *kami*. The priests begin ceremonies by purifying themselves and the space. They have already shut themselves off from the world, eaten special foods, and abstained from sexual intercourse. Then they rinse their mouths and transfer pollutants from themselves to a stick that is thrown away. All this is to prepare for the presence of the *kami*.

At this point the priest calls on the *kami* to attend. Then he leads the presentation of offerings, which include rice, fruits, vegetables, sake, and fish. Prayers of praise to the *kami* are made. After the priest confers the *kami*'s blessing through a branch of a sacred tree, he shares a meal with the *kami*, using the food and drink just offered. The purpose of all this is not so much a specific gift or blessing but the sense of being in harmony with the forces of nature, which the *kami* control.

Most Shinto worship is carried out by individuals in private, but occasionally there are public festivals, conducted by priests. Public festivals are tied to the agricultural year (for example, the Harvest Prayer Festival and the Festival of First Fruits). Big festivals (*matsuri*) are led by priests with formal chants and music, and offerings are made with food and sake.

Private devotion includes the following. A devotee will go to a local shrine, thought to be the special dwelling place of local *kami*. There is usually a stone tank of water, where the person rinses out his mouth for purification before he enters. Often there are small thatched-roof buildings for prayer and meditation. The devotee can make an offering of money in a special box, pull a rope attached to a bell, bow to the shrine, and then pray to the *kami* silently. Then he might buy a printed fortune, which will show him how the *kami* have answered his prayer. He might tie a piece of paper to the branches of a tree to thank the *kami* for the anticipated answer to prayer or prevention of a bad occurrence.

Shinto devotees also worship at a family altar in the home, where the *kami* of their ancestors are revered.

Christian Analysis

It's easy to see that the fundamental beliefs of Shinto are worlds apart from Christian faith. First of all, in Shinto there is no one creator God but a cosmos full of vague spirits called *kami*. Human beings are not sinners but potential *kami* themselves. Our goal in life is to find peace with nature rather than union with a holy God. So there is no way in Shinto to find genuine forgiveness if a Japanese person hears the voice of conscience that cries out, *"There's something wrong! You are not right with your Maker!"*

It's also easy to see how Shinto can lead to idolatry—worshiping one's nation instead of God. Since adherents believe the Sun Goddess chose Japan because she was special, it was easy for them in the 1930s to believe they were superior to the rest of the world and had a divine right to conquer it. Most Japanese have learned from that tragic mistake, but it's a good reminder to us that no nation is ever close to the kingdom of God and that "we must obey God rather than men" (Acts 5:29 NIV).

Islam

*The World's Most Important
Religion Geopolitically*

Islam is the second biggest religion in the world. In 2007 there were 1.36 billion Muslims worldwide. You may be surprised to learn that most do not live in the Middle East. There are 210 million in Indonesia who say Allah is God and Muhammad the chief and seal (last) of the prophets, 150 million in India, 163 million in Pakistan. As you can see, far more Muslims live in South and Southeast Asia than in the Middle East. There are more than 120 million in sub-Saharan Africa, with 67 million in Nigeria alone.

How many Muslims live in the United States? It depends on who answers the question. Scholars at City College of New York say

1.1 million, while the Council on American-Islamic Relations (CAIR), a Muslim organization, claims 6–7 million. The best estimate is probably between one and two million.

The 2007 Pew survey of Muslim Americans found that two-thirds are foreign-born. Among the foreign-born, most have immigrated since 1990. Of the roughly one-third of Muslim Americans who are native born, the majority are converts and African-American.

There are about twelve hundred mosques in the United States, which provides further evidence that the numbers are considerably less than reported by CAIR. If there were actually five million Muslims in the United States (and CAIR claims more), each mosque would serve nearly forty-two hundred Muslims. Yet many mosques are storefronts, and the nation's largest mosque, Dar al-Hijrah near Washington, DC, has only about three thousand weekly attendees.

Islam is one of the world's fastest-growing religions (Christianity is growing almost as quickly). Several factors account for this: Muslims are aggressive in their evangelism (especially in Africa), their message is easily understood (Muslims say Christian theology is complicated and hard to believe), and they offer the politically alienated the prospect of national transformation by changing their nation's civil law to Islamic law (Sharia law). But the most significant factor in Islam's rapid growth rate is birthrate. In 1997 the United Nations estimated that a woman in developed countries typically bore 1.6 children during her lifetime, while the average woman in the largest Muslim countries gave birth to 5.

The Arabic word *Islam* (literally, "submission") points to the central idea of the religion—submission to the total will of Allah. *Allah* is Arabic for "the god." Muslims proclaim to the world that Allah alone is great and rules with absolute control over every atom of the universe. Therefore it only makes sense for each of us to submit every detail of life to Allah's will, as it has been revealed to his final prophet Muhammad.

Muhammad

Muhammad (AD 570–632), the founder of Islam, endured a troubled childhood. He lost his father before he was born, and his mother died when he was six. Then he lived with his grandfather, who perished two years later. The orphan lived out the rest of his childhood with his uncle. Perhaps because of his own heartbreaks, Muhammad became a religious seeker, often retreating to mountain caves above Mecca to meditate.

When he was forty, Muhammad said the angel Gabriel began delivering to him messages from Allah. The first messages terrified Muhammad, but he received reassurance from his wife Khadijah and her Christian cousin, who assured Muhammad that he had been visited by the same being who had visited Moses and that God was calling him to be a prophet to his people. The earliest messages emphasized that there is only one God (before Muhammad the Arab tribes worshiped 360 different gods, the chief of whom had been called Allah) and that every human being will face the judgment of this God. These messages and later revelations, all of which the illiterate Muhammad dictated to his disciples, make up the Qur'an.

Do Christians and Muslims Worship the Same God?

In one sense, Christians and Muslims *do* worship the same God. Since there is only one God, whenever a Muslim makes contact with this God, he is connecting with the Father of Jesus Christ, whether he knows it or not.

But in another sense, they don't. Muslims and Christians have different ideas of what God is like and how to reach him. Muslims agree with Christians that God is one, but they deny his triune nature, his incarnation as Jesus, and Jesus' death and resurrection. They agree that God is all-powerful, but Christians say his power was a vulnerable power (the cross), and he refuses to force his power on people. Jesus says, for example, "I stand at the door and knock. If anyone hears my voice and opens the door, I will come in and eat with him" (Rev. 3:20 NIV).

The Qur'an

The Qur'an is about the same length as the New Testament, but the similarities stop there. It was dictated by only one man (the

New Testament was composed by many writers) and is neither a book of history (like the Gospels and Acts of the Apostles) nor a life of Muhammad (the Gospels aim to provide the theologically significant events of Jesus' life) nor a theological treatise (as Paul's letter to the Romans could be considered). Instead, it is a book of proclamation—that God is one and sovereign, judgment is coming, and we need to submit to Allah.

Inspiration

You can find these themes in the Bible as well, but Muslims and Christians have very different conceptions of the nature of scriptural inspiration. While Christians believe the Bible is a joint product of both human and divine agency, Muslims believe their holy book contains not a shred of human influence. Christians usually want to distinguish Paul's personal writing style or cultural influences from the divine Word, for example, but Muslims deny that Muhammad's personality or cultural affinities had anything to do with the words of the Qur'an. Muslims, then, accept a dictation theory of inspiration that nearly all Christians reject for their Bible. This is one reason why the Muslim community was so outraged by Salman Rushdie's *Satanic Verses*.

The novel insinuates that the Qur'an is not the word of Allah but has been altered by either the angel Gabriel or Muhammad's followers who first recorded the revelations entrusted to the Prophet. Muslims consider the title of the book even more sinister because, according to Islamic tradition, very early versions of the Qur'an contained verses that suggested the worship of three goddesses alongside Allah. Muhammad soon had those verses removed, explaining that the devil had given him disinformation. They have been known ever since in Islamic lore as the "satanic verses." So the implication of Rushdie's title is that the entire Qur'an, which for Muslims is as sacred as the person of

Jesus is to Christians, has been corrupted.

The Message of the Qur'an

The Qur'an tells its readers and listeners (it was meant to be recited aloud) that human beings are created by Allah to serve him and avoid idolatry, which would mean giving first allegiance to anything other than God—money, family, race, success, or earthly life itself.

There are two final destinations—hell (which punishes with boiling water, pus, chains, searing wind, and food that chokes) for people who reject the message of the Prophet, and Paradise, which offers wide-eyed damsels, wine, and luscious fruits to those who prove to be faithful

Muslims (and comparable delights to females). Modernist Muslims say the same thing about these passages that many Christians say about biblical descriptions of heaven and hell—they are simply metaphorical ways of saying that the presence of God is delightful and absence from him will be horrible.

The Qur'an teaches that Islam is the simplest and clearest religion and stands as the essential core of every other religion. It is the revelation that was given originally to Abraham but was later distorted by the Jewish and Christian traditions. This is the reason Allah needed to give it once more to Muhammad.

Every act a Muslim engages in should be an act of worship that seeks to please God. Based on the Islamic concept of *tawhid* (oneness), acts of worship cannot be classified as public or private because God's angels record all deeds. Thus the Muslim should always be God-conscious, which should affect his or her behavior. The Holy Qur'an's *Surah* 107—Neighborly Needs—contains only seven short verses but gives guidance to the Muslim on worshiping in a holistic God-conscious manner.

While the *Surah* places special emphasis on providing assistance to two marginalized groups in human society (orphans and the hungry), Muslims are also encouraged to engage in small acts of kindness that benefit God's creation. For instance, within the past week I have (1) visited a friend taking chemotherapy, (2) picked up the mail and newspapers of a neighbor on vacation, and (3) watered my outdoor plants and flowers, thirsty in the July sun. All of these acts satisfy the requirements outlined in this *Surah*.

When I attend Jummah Prayer on Friday, I pray in front of both Muslims and non-Muslims. The *Surah* reminds us to be sincere in our prayer and not pray to be seen by others. Only then will one's prayers earn God's bounty.

Reginald Shareef, Ph.D.
Radford University, Department of Political Science
Virginia Tech, Center for Public Administration and Policy

Jesus in Islam

Usually American Christians are surprised when they learn of the extraordinary respect that Muslims hold for Jesus. He was the greatest of all the prophets, they say, until Muhammad. The Qur'an even calls Jesus "Messiah," "word from God," "a Spirit from God," and the son of Mary who was "strengthened with the Holy Spirit." It teaches the virgin birth (Muslims say Mary was the purest woman in all creation) and accepts the historicity of all the Gospel miracles, except for Jesus' resurrection.

How Jews and Christians Went Wrong

Muslims regard the Old and New Testaments as the Word of God, but they quickly add that Jews and Christians have corrupted the texts at critical points. Jews perverted the original revelation, Muslims claim, by an act of communal narcissism. They took a message intended for every nation and turned it into an exclusive proclamation of salvation for themselves, saying they alone are the chosen people. Although the Qur'an is silent on the issue, some Muslims believe that Jews substituted Isaac's name for Ishmael's in the book of Genesis and thus concealed for centuries the Arabian connection in the history of salvation.

Muslims believe that Christians made the mistake of turning Jesus into a God and therefore reverting to the polytheism that Allah forbids. Most Muslims deny that Jesus was crucified, because the Qur'an states that the Jews did not kill Jesus and that God "raised [Jesus] to himself" in a manner reminiscent of Elijah. More important, Muslims deny that Jesus was the Son of God, assuming this would mean that God had engaged in sex, which is unimaginable. Islam also denies that Jesus was a Savior because of its conviction that each of us must be responsible for our own sins. To imagine that someone else can save us from our sins seems to Muslims to be spiritually irresponsible. Most of them are convinced that no one can receive such spiritual benefits from another. I say "most" because many mystical Muslims (Sufis) believe they need the help of the Prophet and his family for salvation.

Muslim tradition teaches that eventually both Judaism and Christianity will wither away, as most of the world accepts Islam's version of monotheism. Almost all Muslims believe that Jesus will indeed return, as Christians believe, but when he comes, he will turn the world back to the original teaching of Abraham—Islam.

The Five Pillars

These are the five practices that every faithful Muslim wants to observe.

1. *Profession of faith:* "There is no god but Allah, and Muhammad is the messenger of Allah." Simply reciting this in public makes one a Muslim. Notice how important Muhammad is. Many Muslims believe he never sinned and performed many miracles, though there is no record of these in the Qur'an. His sayings and deeds, recorded with varying degrees of authenticity in the *Hadith* (many volumes), contain miracle stories. These sayings and deeds, after being weighed for their relative authenticity, serve as precedents for Islamic law (Sharia). At the same time, Muslims insist that Muhammad was only a man.

2. *Prayer five times daily.* Believers are to face Mecca and pray in the early morning, at noon, midafternoon, sunset, and in the evening. But before prayer at each of these times, there is to be washing of the arms, feet, mouth, and nostrils—and three times for each of these body parts. The prayers are generally set prayers of praise and adoration. Every Friday there is a prayer service at the mosque (though Friday is not a holy day as Sunday is for Christians and Saturday for Jews), with two sermons by trained laymen. Women sit separately from the men, but most women do not attend.

3. *Almsgiving.* Sunnis give 2.5 percent of their income to support Muslim needy, but Shi'ites are told to contribute 20 percent. (See below for the differences between these two groups.)

4. *Fasting during Ramadan.* Ramadan is a month in the Islamic calendar, which is based on the moon, and so the month is at a different time from year to year. It marks the time when the Qur'an was first revealed to Muhammad. During this month Muslims are to abstain from all liquids, food, tobacco, and sex between first light in the morning and full darkness at night. They say the purpose of this fasting is to practice self-restraint.

5. *Pilgrimage to Mecca.* Muslims believe Mecca (in today's Saudi Arabia) is the navel of the world, the location of Eden, and the point on planet Earth closest to Paradise. Here they say Abraham,

Hagar, and Ishmael built a house of worship, which still exists as a giant stone cube, draped in black. It was also from here that Muhammad is said to have taken his "night journey" to Jerusalem

and then to Paradise and back—all in one night. Some Muslims say this is allegorical not literal. Few Muslims actually make the pilgrimage to Mecca; they are blamed only if they can afford the trip and are healthy enough to go.

Sunnis and Shi'ites

Since September 11, 2001, most Americans have heard of Sunnis and Shi'ites but have little idea of what makes them different. Here are the essentials.

Sunnis are far and away the most numerous, representing about 85 percent of all Muslims in the world. Their interpretation of the faith is based on what the *ulama* have said. These are the Islamic scholars who have reached consensus on what is true and right, based on their understanding of the Qur'an and *Hadith*—the collected record of what the Prophet said and did. Sunnis think revelation stopped with the decisions of the early *ulama* centuries ago and that their consensus judgments were infallible. Some modernist Muslims blame Islamic radicalism on this belief in infallibility. They say the *ulama* should never have taken away Muslims' right to think independently (*ijtihad*), based on the Qur'an and Islamic law.

Sunnis also believe Muhammad did not designate a successor, and so the first leaders (caliphs) after the Prophet were legitimately chosen by the early Islamic community. Shi'ites disagree with this, as you will see.

Sunnis have generally had the upper hand in Islamic history, so they have an optimistic view of history. They believe Islam is steadily growing and winning ascendancy in the world. The last fifty years, in which Muslim nations have found great oil wealth under their sands, seems to have confirmed this view for many.

Shi'ites, on the other hand, comprise only 15 percent of the world's Muslims and live mostly in Iran and southern Iraq. They get their name from the battles over Muhammad's successor, after which they split from the majority to form their own distinct party (*Shia*). Shi'ites believe Muhammad's successor should have come from his family and that the Prophet had chosen Ali, his cousin and son-in-law. But since the Muslim community chose Abu Bakr and several other caliphs from outside the family, Shi'ites consider three of the first four caliphs (one was Ali) to have been illegitimate.

The most important event in Shia history was the martyrdom in AD 680 of Ali's son Hussein, who led an uprising against one of the "illegitimate" caliphs. Hussein has become the Shi'ite symbol of resistance to tyranny, and to this day participation in the annual reenactment of his martyrdom is the central act of Shi'ite piety.

The largest group within the Shi'ite faith is known as the Twelvers. They believe the leader who stood at the end of Muhammad's line, the Twelfth Imam (prayer leader), is still alive invisibly and is going to return visibly at the end of history to rid the world of evil. The president of Iran, Mahmoud Ahmadinejad, has said publicly that the purpose of the Iranian revolution (started in 1979 by the Ayatollah Kohmeini) is to pave the way for the Mahdi's (the "Guided One" or redeemer) return.

UCLA law professor Khaled Abou El Fadl survived torture in Egypt and fled to the United States. He publicly condemned the September 11 attacks and says the real clash involving Islam is not between civilizations but within Islam itself.

El Fadl calls for a "pluralistic, tolerant, and nonviolent Islam." He says Islam stands on two foundational truths—mercy and moderation. These are the key concepts of the Qur'an, and should be the lenses through which one reads the Qur'an. He blames Wahhabis, bankrolled by Saudi oil, for terrorism and calls on the Muslim "silent majority" to rescue the soul of Islam from a "militant and fanatic minority."

El Fadl receives death threats for criticizing what he calls "puritans" and their narrow reading of the Qur'an.

Other prominent Shi'ite leaders, however, disagree. Iraq's Ayatollah Ali al-Sistani teaches that the Mahdi's coming cannot be hastened by human activity.

For most of their history, Shi'ites have been powerless, marginalized, and oppressed—often by Sunnis. They have not held much hope for the growth of their movement in this world. Therefore their recent success in the Iranian revolution (1979–present) and now in Iraq, and the hope of some for the early return of the Mahdi, is fairly new.

Islam and Violence

Some have attributed the horror of September 11 to Islamic jihad, which is usually translated as "holy war." But this is misleading. Muslims divide jihad into two categories: the greater and the lesser. The greater jihad is the war within oneself against one's own evil. The lesser jihad is defense against aggressive attacks on Islam. These actions do not necessarily involve armed conflict but may simply be expressed with the pen or tongue. While radical Islam today thinks jihad should be carried to all the world, mainstream Islam through most of its history has said that armed conflict is to be primarily defensive and strictly regulated.

Muhammad wrote:

> Fight in the way of God against those who fight against you, but begin not hostilities. Lo! God loveth not aggressors. . . . There is no compulsion in religion. . . . God forbids you not, with regard to those who fight you not for [your] religion nor drive you out of your homes, from dealing kindly and justly with them.[1]

The first Muslim leader after Muhammad, Abu Bakr, wrote:

> I instruct you in ten matters: Do not kill women, children, the old, or the infirm; do not cut down fruit-bearing trees; do not destroy any town; do not kill sheep or camels except for the purposes of eating; do not burn date trees or submerge them; do not steal from the booty and do not be cowardly.[2]

The Qur'an says that if you kill one person without reason, it is as if you slay all of humanity (5:32). At the same time, the Qur'an commands its readers to "slay the idolaters wheresoever you find them" (9:5). Some Muslim scholars say this was a command given in the heat of the first community's struggle for survival, and they point to passages in the Qur'an, such as the famous one condemning religious coercion in 2:256: "There is [should be] no compulsion in religion." They also say the Qur'an promotes religious diversity, such as 5:48: "To each of you [peoples] We [God] have given a law and a way and a pattern of life. If God had pleased He could surely have made you one people (professing one faith). But He wished to try and test you by that which He gave you." This is the translation in the Princeton University Press edition of the Qur'an, and the phrase "professing one faith" is not in the Arabic. This edition's translator thinks it is implied, and that is the interpretation that El Fadl (see sidebar on Muslim dissent) and other Muslim "liberals" see in this and similar passages (11:118–19; 49:13).

But while many Muslims condemn the terrorism used by their militant coreligionists, there is a historical link between Islam and aggressive military and political action. Muhammad was a military and political—as well as religious—leader. He served as both Prophet and commander, preacher and soldier, Imam and magistrate. The first community of Muslims was a sociopolitico-religious amalgamation, and traditional Islam has taught that government should enforce Islamic or Sharia law, which is why Islam has usually shown greater organic unity between this world's and otherworldly concerns than is seen in Christianity. Sometimes Muslim leaders have exploited passages, such as "slay the idolaters" (as well as the

Islamic teaching that warriors who die in a holy war will go straight to Paradise and skip over years of suffering in a purgatory-like existence), when they have tried to muster a people for war.

Islam and the West

While only a minority of Muslims express strong contempt for the West ("America is the Great Satan," for example), many Muslims regard the West with ambivalence. They appreciate and use its technology, but consider Western culture as a threat to their own because it represents modernization without moral control. Muslims place great emphasis on the integrity of the nuclear family and pride themselves on the stability of their families. They see our Western values of atomistic individualism and sexual permissiveness as destructive to family life. They are fully aware of America's soaring rates of divorce, abortion, pornography, crime, and chemical addiction (much of which is broadcast to their countries through movies, TV, and the Internet) and wonder why Americans regard Muslim culture with self-righteous disdain.

Also Muslims tend to view the West, particularly the United States, as irreligious and godless because of our separation of church and state. If God is sovereign over the cosmos, Muslims argue, then every aspect of life—including the state—ought to come under the rule of his laws. Islamic law (Sharia) should therefore serve as a set of fundamental principles informing the laws of every nation on earth.

More militant Muslims feel the West is out to destroy Islam (despite the fact that the last few major American interventions abroad, in Kuwait, Somalia, the Balkans, and even Iraq were conducted in defense of Muslims). A Western-educated Muslim engineer once asked me (before Pakistan's acquisition of nuclear weapons), "Why does the United States permit India, Israel, and South Africa to have nuclear weapons but not Iraq or Pakistan?" Many Muslims believe there is a Zionist-American conspiracy to reduce the Middle Eastern nations to their former colonial status under Western domination. They see Israel as America's client state and believe that Jewish lobbies dictate American government policy. As the war in Iraq has progressed, more and more Muslims have concluded the United States is out to control oil and the Middle East.

Yet these suspicions fall far short of the venomous hatred required to teach young men to fly jetliners as missiles into skyscrapers, killing thousands of innocent people. The genesis of this barbarity lies not with Islam but *Islamism*, the term some scholars use to distinguish mainstream Islam from the twentieth-century terroristic ideology first seen in the Ayatollah Khomeini.

According to Paul Marshall, British-born expert in international religious conflict, America is not first on the list of things bin Laden hates. First is his own country, Saudi Arabia, for cozying up to the Western powers and allowing American troops to be stationed on sacred soil, where Muhammad received his revelations. Second are the moderate Arab governments, such as Egypt, Jordan, and Malaysia, that bin Laden feels have sold out to the West. Third are those who in his view oppress Muslims, including Israel, Russia (because of Chechnya), India (because of Kashmir), America, and several other countries.

Marshall says that bin Laden figures he cannot do anything about the first two groups because America is protecting them. So America, their bodyguard, must be destroyed first. The official name for bin Laden's Al-Qaeda is "World Islamic Front for Holy War against Jews and Crusaders." Al-Qaeda considers Jews to be allies with the Christian West and sees America and Europe as crusaders, continuing the medieval Crusades of conquest and pillaging of Muslim countries. Bin Laden thinks that Jews control these "Christian" countries by their influence on American media and government. Al-Qaeda's aims, then, are twofold: to impose its distorted version of Islam on the Muslim world, and then to impose this Islamism on the rest of the world.

Islamism is preferred by many scholars to the popular term *Islamic fundamentalism*, which was coined by the Western media and used to denigrate conservative Christians ("fundamentalists") in the West by associating them with Islamic violence. In the *New York Times Magazine*, Jeffrey Goldberg described the way proponents of Islamism take boys as young as eight years old out of dire poverty and put them in special schools, isolated from all secular learning, art, music, women, and mainstream Islam. There they are indoctrinated, day in and day out in the theology, ethics, and worldview of violent Islamism. There is no consideration of different views of the Qur'an, only simple rote learning of prescribed views, and liberal doses of venomous anti-Semitism. A worldwide terroristic network gives these boys an education at no cost to them—paying for their room and board, clothing, teachers, and buildings, and then giving them jobs in organizations like the Taliban.[3]

Your Muslim Neighbor

Perhaps you have a Muslim neighbor or co-worker and have wondered how to befriend him or her and encourage an openness to the gospel. How do you share the love of Christ with Muslims? Here are a few ideas.

1. Show real interest in your Muslim neighbor's faith. Study it. This chapter is a good start.

2. Be slow to criticize. A recent Muslim convert to Christian faith in India said, "Don't discuss any of the faults or weaknesses of Islam or speak ill of Muhammad or the Qur'an. Speak to the Muslim of Jesus and his stories and miracles." You may be surprised to learn that Jesus is the most developed character in the Qur'an. As we saw earlier in this chapter, Muslims typically have huge respect for Jesus. Build on this respect and ask your friend if he'd like to read the *Injil* (New Testament) to learn more about Jesus.

3. Muslims have a very difficult time understanding how Jesus could be God. To them it seems polytheistic or even blasphemous to say God has a Son. As we've seen, most Muslims think this would require God to have engaged in sex, which is unthinkable. But you can explain that Christians agree that God did not engage in sex, that even the Qur'an calls Jesus the Messiah (Qur'an 3:45),

and the Gospels say he is Lord and claimed the authority to forgive sins. Only God has that authority.

4. The incarnation is equally difficult for Muslims. Charles White, a missionary to Muslim parts of Africa, used to tell his students about the man who became an ant. He saw ants going into a house where they would be poisoned. He told them over and over not to enter, but they didn't listen. Finally, the man became an ant so the other ants could hear and understand. By becoming one of them, this man was able to save ants from destruction. This story helped Muslims understand why God became a man in Jesus Christ.

5. The incarnation might be a bit easier for Shi'ites to understand because they believe a divine substance from Muhammad passes from Imam to Imam. They can be told that in a similar way the divine substance passed—as it were—from the Father to the Son.

6. White also told his Muslim students of two kinds of great-

Muslim feminists (yes, there are some) say Islam was egalitarian at the beginning and point to evidence of this in the Qur'an. They are encouraged by what Muhammad did for women—banning the then-prevalent female infanticide, and insisting on a woman's rights to property ownership, inheritance, education, and divorce. They point to Khadijah, Muhammad's first wife, who was a businesswoman, and his later wives, who taught both men and women in Medina.

Also they lament many current practices in Islam, which they say come from tribal culture not the Qur'an: honor killings; dress codes, including veils and burkas that cover everything except the eyes; rapes that often result in punishment for the victim because of a rule that four witnesses are required to accuse the man; restrictions on the ability of women to travel; and fewer rights for women in marriage, divorce, legal status, and education.

Most Muslims say that gender relations in Islam are based on religious and moral equality but complementarity in roles, with men's space being the public realm and women's space being the home. They concede that the Qur'an allows rebellious wives to be beaten (4:34) and that the legal status of a woman's testimony is half that of a man's.

The status of women in Islam is complex. In Iran women's rights are limited, yet there are women legislators in Parliament and 60 percent of university students are women. Under the Taliban in Afghanistan, women were forced into seclusion, could not work outside the home, could not be educated after the age of eight, and could not see a male doctor.

ness. One kind is seen in the king who sits on a high throne and has scores of servants scurrying around to do his bidding. The other kind of greatness is seen in a brilliant student who works hard in medical school and graduates with the ability to go anywhere he wants. But rather than following other top graduates to lucrative practices in the suburbs, he goes to work among the poor in the inner city. That is what God did, in his power and greatness, when he came to live among sinful men.

7. The message of forgiveness and power through the Holy Spirit can be appealing to a Muslim who feels crushed by the demands of the law. She is told that she can never know for sure if she will reach Paradise, and because she knows the weakness of her heart, she is in despair. The gospel message that Christ came to save sinners, not the righteous, and that he gives power to live a righteous life nonetheless can be liberating for such a conscientious soul.

8. Like all our neighbors, our Muslim neighbors and friends should be shown respect and love. We should recognize the religious truth they already have and not assume they would need to throw out everything they've ever believed to come to Christ. If they sense your respect for them, they may, like Cornelius who already feared God and prayed regularly to God before he heard about Jesus (Acts 10:2), "listen to all that the Lord has commanded you to say" (v. 33).

8

Two Common Questions

They say you shouldn't discuss politics or religion at the dinner table with guests, but sometimes your guests start talking about these things anyway, and there's not much you can do. Perhaps before you read this book, you felt unequipped for discussing either your own Christian faith or (especially) the world religions. But now after reading this book, you'll feel much more confident to wade into such heavy conversation.

Let me try to give you just a bit more help before we close this little tutorial. I find that when it comes to Christians and other religions, there are two basic questions on which different kinds of Christians take opposing sides. Now there are many different kinds of Christians, but for the sake of talk about world religions, I am going to narrow the groups down to two: liberal Christians and conservative Christians. I won't bother to define these terms in any detail—that would be another book—but let me say that when these two questions about the religions come up, and they often do, these two big blocs of Christians tend to answer them in diametrically opposed ways.

So here are the two questions—each is directed at a different group. Of liberal Christians I ask, Can or should we try to evangelize members of other religions? Of conservative Christians I ask, Can we ever learn anything from other religions?

Generally (there are exceptions of course), liberal Christians think we should dialogue with people of other faiths, but they rule out any effort to convert them. That's usually because most liberal Christians think all the other religions eventually lead to God. In a metaphor they use often, they describe the different religions as just different roads leading up the sides of the same mountain, and they all converge at the top.

Generally (there are exceptions here as well), conservative Christians think the only reason we should talk to members of other religions about religion is to try to convert them. They think it would be fine to make friends with, say, a Buddhist co-worker, but if the conversation moves to religion, it must lead to debate and then conversion. What other approach could you take, they reason, when everything about the Buddhist's religion is from the devil? That's the case for every religion except Christianity and Judaism. Everything in the other religions is demonic.

So, there are two questions, and each is directed at a different group. To liberal Christians, I ask if we can or should try to evangelize members of other religions. And to conservative Christians, I ask if we can ever learn anything from other religions.

Should We Evangelize People in Other Religions?

Typically, liberals have several objections to trying to evangelize members of other faiths. Often liberals believe that people of other religions are already saved in their own way, since all religions have the same goal, thus leading to God.

There are several problems with this belief, however. First of all, it is not at all clear that the world's religions share the same goal. Theravadin Buddhists do not believe in God, and so have no desire to meet him. The same is true for disciples of Advaita Vedanta (Hindu), who believe they are one with Brahman. They don't believe in a personal God either and are seeking the end of individual existence. These goals are light-years from what Christians seek—union as individuals in love with the three persons of the Trinity. Each of these religions has its own mountain, and each peak is very different and far away from the others.

Another problem is that the New Testament makes it very clear that union with the Trinity comes only by Jesus Christ. Jesus said, "No one comes to the Father except through me" (John 14:6). Peter declared, "There is salvation in no one else, for there is no other name under heaven given among mortals by which we must be saved" (Acts 4:12). John announced, "God has given us eternal life, and this life is in his Son. He who has the Son has life; he who does not have the Son of God does not have life" (1 John 5:11–12 NIV).

As far as the apostles were concerned, there is no other Savior and no other way to God but through Jesus. There is no salvation through other religions. There is no way to the true God except by knowing Jesus Christ. No other religion, only the faith of Jesus and the apostles, gets a person to the true God. Now some theologians in the early church thought people in other religions might be saved, but it would be in spite of their religions not because of them. And it would be only through the life and death of Jesus, and by accepting the gospel in some way and time that God only knows—at the point of death or in the millennium or some other way. In other words, they would have to recognize that their religion was not the way to the fullness of God, that only Jesus is. For more on this, see my book *God's Rivals*.[1]

So the first answer to this question is that a person of another faith will never get to the triune God through her religion, and we need to evangelize her. She needs to hear the good news of Jesus. This alone will get her all the way to the true God.

The second answer is that Jesus himself told all of us who follow him to "make disciples of all nations" (Matt. 28:19). This is a command that he repeated several times (Mark 13:10; 16:15; Acts 1:8).

Some liberal Christians might say, "But some non-Christians have so much truth already." True enough. But they still don't know the Savior. Knowing part of the truth is a far cry from knowing Truth incarnate. If we know that people in a village are slowly dying from impure water that is nevertheless keeping them alive for some years, we won't be satisfied that they have water and are still alive. We will want to get them pure water to stop the dying process. The same is true in religion. We will want everyone, even those who have some water, to get the pure Water of Life that brings wholeness in this life and salvation in the one to come. Lydia in Philippi was already worshiping God, but Paul made sure she heard and accepted the gospel so that she might know the true God in all his fullness—Jesus Christ (Acts 16:14).

Now by evangelism I don't mean proselytizing, which is often coercive, rude, and insensitive. No, true evangelism is when we take the time to make a lasting friendship, listen to our friend's perspective, offer loving help where it is needed, and humbly and respectfully share the gospel when the Spirit opens the door—not before. I say "humbly" because we may know we have the truth in Jesus but we must acknowledge that we see him only in part and follow him imperfectly. Having Jesus is not the same as knowing him in full or following him fully. I say "respectfully" because we should talk with our non-Christian friend after we have studied his religion, seen what truth is there, and tried to represent it fairly. Of course every truth in another religion (such as the idea that there is a God who is personal) will be essentially different from the Christian version that is centered in Jesus. But it is still a truth, if only partial, nonetheless.

Can We Learn from Other Religions?

The conservative Christian's tendency is to think that all the religions are demonic and therefore can offer nothing of value. Therefore many conservatives would see little or no use in dialoguing with people of other religions except for the purpose of evangelizing. If the other religions have come completely from below, they couldn't have any truth. So what's the point of talking, unless we're trying to persuade them that the only truth is in Christianity?

The trouble with this view is that it can't be squared with the Bible. Take the apostle Paul, for example, who was the premier evangelist and missionary of the New Testament. He told the pagans in Athens (Acts 17) that their own poets had truth, and they had some connection—even if remote—to God. In other words, the Athenian pagans, while mired in religious ignorance, were nevertheless groping for the same God whom Paul knew to be the Father of Jesus Christ. He tells them, "What therefore you worship as unknown, this I proclaim to you" (17:23). That is, their ideas about God were nearly all wrong, but the object of their misguided worship was still the same God who had revealed himself to Paul as the true and living God.

Paul quoted some of their own poets: "For 'in him we live and move and have our being'; as even some of your own poets have said, 'For we too are his offspring'" (v. 28).

Paul was probably quoting Epimenides (sixth century BC) and Aratus (fourth century BC). The astonishing thing here is that

Paul, who apparently believed that Greek religion was abysmally ignorant of the true God, still conceded—in a sermon highlighting Greek religious ignorance!—that the religions had *some* access to *some* true notions of the living God.

Some conservatives might object and ask, "Are you saying these pagans are saved simply because they have religious truth?" My answer is, "Not at all." The Bible is full of people outside of the kingdom of God who nevertheless have parts of the truth of God. Think of Balaam, the pagan prophet who eventually led Israel into immorality and idolatry (Rev. 2:14). Yet the Holy Spirit used him to prophesy the truth about the future of Israel (Numbers 24). The Egyptian king Neco was another. He is never singled out for moral or religious virtue, yet the Bible says God spoke through Neco and was displeased that Josiah did not listen to the word of God that came through this pagan king (2 Chron. 35:20–27).

Now that doesn't mean that Christians can learn from non-Christian religions something that contradicts the truths passed down by the historic orthodox church, or that we would learn something new that is not already contained in holy Scripture. But it does mean that we might *see* something in the Bible we had never seen before, or at least we might see it in a different way.

This has happened many times in church history. One of the first was in the debates of the second through the fourth centuries over Jesus' relations to the Father and the Spirit. It was only by using concepts and categories from Greek philosophy—which was a religion of its own—that the early church was able to formulate the doctrine of the Trinity. The raw materials of the doctrine were in the Bible already, but it was by learning from another philosophical-religious system that those raw materials could be understood in a systematic way.

We can also learn from people in other religions. I remember Khaled, whom I met in Jerusalem at a conference of Jews, Muslims, and Christians to talk about peace and the land of Israel. We disagreed a lot, made a tiny bit of headway, and forged some friendships. Khaled Abu Ras was a very brave twenty-six-year-old Arabic teacher from Nazareth who looked ten years older. In 2001 he and ten other Muslims founded the Prophetic Tradition Helpers Association, a moderate Muslim attempt to oppose Muslim militancy and extremism. As one rabbi, who was familiar with the group, told the *Jerusalem Post*, this effort by Muslim moderates to speak publicly against Muslim extremists was "very impressive, very brave, and very dangerous." When I asked Khaled if he was afraid, he replied with a smile, "Every one of us will die at the time God decides and not one day before." I was glad to see that he was still alive in the spring of 2007.

The bravery of this man from another religion has inspired me to try to be more courageous in my own Christian life. When I think of how I am hesitant to make public arguments, which I know will be criticized, I remember Khaled and his willingness to *die* for the sake of the truth he professes publicly—because of his faith in Allah. The worst I ever suffer is public contempt, but Khaled faces the possibility of death. I don't share his faith in Allah, but the courage it produces inspires my faith in Jesus to go deeper.

We can also learn from other religious *practices*. In the introduction to this book, I talked about the Dalai Lama's forgiveness of the Chinese for murdering his Tibetan people. We Christians see forgiveness through the prism of Jesus forgiving his executioners, which is different from Tibetan Buddhist reasons for forgiveness. But this real-life practice of forgiveness can motivate us to look more closely at our Christian duty to forgive our enemies.

Then there's the Muslim practice of prayer five times daily, and this prayer is mostly praise, not asking for things. There's nothing wrong with asking for things, since the Lord's Prayer instructs us to do so, but too often we spend far too little time in praise, not to mention too little time in prayer period. We can learn from Muslims the importance of having set times for prayer, instead of relying on our own fickle sense of when we have the time and inclination to pray.

One Last Word

Let me close with a final word about our relations with men and women of other faiths. Paul said our real battle is not against flesh and blood but "against the cosmic powers of this present darkness" (Eph. 6:12). That means we should be wary of looking on people of other religions as our enemies. Our only real enemies—besides sin, the flesh, and the devil—are the devil's soldiers whom the Bible calls "principalities and powers." These are spiritual beings who war against God's kingdom and sometimes use other religions to mask their own designs. Also they wage war within the church, sometimes pitting Christian disciples against one another.

This means our witness as Christians to members of other religions should involve patient conversation not hostile argument, plenty of listening and befriending before any attempt to persuade. (There may be exceptions to this, such as when there is a public forum in which Christianity is being misrepresented, and we need to speak up before we have a chance to make friends.) It means loving witness to others who sincerely believe they have the truth. We may believe they have been deceived by spiritual forces, but we must also be humble in our sharing, acknowledging that while the truth has grabbed us, we neither know it in full nor (usually) live it well.

Notes

Introduction

1. David B. Barrett and Todd M. Johnson, *International Bulletin of Missionary Research* 31:1 (January 2007), 32.

2. Peter Berger, "Epistemological Modesty: An Interview with Peter Berger," *Christian Century* (October 29, 1997), 972–78.

Chapter 1 Hinduisms

1. Actually, Buddhism was started in what is now Nepal, which is very close to India, and developed in and around India in its first centuries. See chapter 3 for an introduction to Buddhism.

Chapter 2 Judaism

1. And of course, the first Christians were Jews as well.

2. Milton Steinberg, *Basic Judaism* (New York: Harcourt, Brace, 1947).

3. Jacob Neusner, *A Rabbi Talks with Jesus* (Montreal: McGill-Queen's University Press, 2000).

Chapter 3 Buddhism

1. Dalai Lama and Howard C. Cutler, *The Art of Happiness: A Handbook for Living* (New York: Riverhead Books, 1998).

2. C. S. Lewis, *The Abolition of Man* (London: Oxford University Press, 1943).

3. "Shinran's Confession" in *Buddhism, a Religion of Infinite Compassion: Selections from Buddhist Literature*, ed. Clarence H. Hamilton (New York: Liberal Arts Press, 1952), 141–42.

Chapter 4 Confucianism and Daoism

1. Thomas Merton, *The Way of Chuang Tzu 31; Taote Ching 72; Chuang Tzu 18.1; Chuang Tzu 24.12.*

2. Quoted in Hans Küng and Julia Ching, *Christianity and Chinese Religions* (New York: Doubleday, 1989), 141.

Chapter 5 Christianity

1. See K. S. Latourette, *A History of Christianity* (New York: Harper, 1953), 104–8.

Chapter 7 Islam

1. Qur'an 2: 190; 2: 256; 60: 8.

2. Malik's *Muwatta,' Kitab al-Jihad.*

3. Jeffrey Goldberg, "Inside Jihad U.: The Education of a Holy Warrior," *New York Times Magazine* (June 25, 2000), 25.

Chapter 8 Two Common Questions

1. Gerald R. McDermott, *God's Rivals: Why Has God Allowed Different Religions? Insights from the Bible and the Early Church* (Downers Grove, IL: InterVarsity, 2007).

Glossary

Advaita Vedanta—lit., the "non-dual [system based on] the end of the Vedas"; teaches the way of knowledge to *moksha*.

agnostic—from the Greek word for "I do not know"; a person who doesn't know if there is a god.

ahimsa—noninjury, the center of Gandhi's version of Hinduism.

asceticism—depriving oneself of the pleasures of the flesh—good food and drink, a soft bed, the comforts of family life.

atheist—someone who says, "I know there is no god."

atman—Hindu word for the human self or soul.

avatar—a god who is the incarnation of a chief Hindu god such as Vishnu; the most popular avatar is Krishna.

bar mitzvah—Jewish coming-of-age ceremony for boys at age thirteen; girls go through a bat mitzvah at age twelve.

bhakti—devotion (love and surrender) to a personal Hindu god—one of the four Hindu ways to *moksha*.

bodhisattva—a being on the way to Buddha-hood who steps back into the world of time to rescue others; key concept for *Mahayana* Buddhism.

Brahma—the creator Hindu god, the first in the "Hindu trinity."

Brahman—the Hindu word for the impersonal essence and spirit of the cosmos, which never changes and is one with all that is; in fact all *is* Brahman.

Brahmin—the highest Hindu caste.

caliph—one of the first leaders of Islam after the Prophet.

Chanukah—The Jewish Festival of Lights in December to celebrate the taking of the temple back from the Syrian Greeks by the Maccabees in 142 BC.

ch'i—one of the fundamental substances of the cosmos that gives life and vitality, according to much of Chinese thought.

Conservative Judaism—a branch of American Judaism today, theologically similar to *Reform* but more traditional in its liturgy.

Dao—lit., the Way; used by Confucius for the right way to live and by Daoists for the invisible principle driving the cosmos (formerly spelled Tao).

Filial piety—the centerpiece of Confucian ethics, teaching sons to revere their fathers.

Gnosticism—from the Greek word for "knowledge"; an ancient Christian heresy that taught salvation by special knowledge rather than the cross and resurrection of Jesus.

Hadith—multivolume collection of the sayings and deeds of Muhammad; the basis for *Sharia* law.

Hanukah—see *Chanukah*.

Hasidism—Orthodox pietistic movement in Judaism emphasizing the "rebbe" or mystical leader.

ijtihad—independent thinking based on the *Qur'an* and Islamic law.

Imam—Muslim leader for prayer.

incarnation—lit., "in the flesh"; refers to a god coming into human flesh; only Christians can point to an incarnation in recorded history.

jen—Chinese Confucianist word for "benevolence."

jihad—lit., "struggle"; the greater jihad is against sin in the soul, while the lesser jihad is armed struggle against the enemies of Islam.

jnana—lit., "knowledge"; one of the four main ways to *moksha* in Hindu religions.

Kabbalah—mystical tradition in Judaism that teaches emanations from God that become the world.

kami—the Japanese word for divinities of nature, nation, and localities; some are deified emperors and heroes.

karma—lit., "deeds"; human actions, good and bad, that are rewarded and punished by an impersonal law of the cosmos.

Koran—see *Qur'an*.

kosher—Jewish dietary rules.

logos—the ancient Stoic word for the organizing principle of the cosmos.

Mahayana—largest Buddhist school of teaching; many believe in personal gods called buddhas and *bodhisattvas*.

maya—"illusion" in Sanskrit.

moksha—lit., "liberation" from *samsara*, the goal of almost every Hindu religion.

mysticism—experiencing God or the divine directly, rather than merely hearing or learning or thinking about divine things.

Neoplatonism—the philosophical system of Plotinus and his followers that influenced Augustine, Jonathan Edwards, and many other Christian theologians and emphasized emanation from God and then return by repentance and contemplation, plus the idea that God's thoughts are the real substances behind the "shadows" of matter.

nirvana—the "blowing out" of desire that Buddhists seek; a state of no beings, consciousness, or desire.

Orthodox—lit., "correct belief"; used for (1) the most conservative branch of American Judaism, (2) the mainstream Christian theological and ethical tradition, and (3) the branch of Christianity known more fully as Eastern Orthodox.

pantheism—lit., "all is God"; the idea that God and the world are one and the same.

Passover—Jewish weeklong holiday in the spring to mark the exodus from Egypt.

prasada—Hindu word for the grace of a god.

Qur'an—the Islamic scripture, believed by Muslims to have been revealed to

Muhammad verbatim through the angel Gabriel.

Ramadan—the month of fasting for Muslims to commemorate the time when Muhammad received his first revelations; since the Muslim calendar is lunar, it rotates through the months from year to year.

Reformed—a theological tradition in Christianity stemming from John Calvin and his views, emphasizing sanctification and the sovereignty of God; best known for belief in predestination.

Reform Judaism—the most liberal of the three main Jewish movements in America; the others are *Conservative* and *Orthodox*.

Rosh Hashanah—Jewish New Year.

samsara—the endless cycle of life, death, and rebirth; often called reincarnation by Westerners.

sannyasi[n]—Hindu holy man living a life of *asceticism* and meditation, seeking enlightenment.

satori—enlightenment in *Zen* Buddhism.

Sharia—Islamic law.

Shi'ites—Muslims of the Shi'a branch, found mostly in Iran and southern Iraq, who believe Ali was appointed the first *caliph* (leader).

Sufis—Islamic mystics, found among both *Sunnis* and *Shi'ites*.

Sunnis—the largest group of Muslims (85 percent), who believe revelation stopped with the *Qur'an* and authority was given to Islamic religious scholars long ago.

surah—a chapter in the *Qur'an*.

Talmud—a huge collection of rabbinic commentaries on *Torah* and its traditions.

Tanakh—Jewish word for what Christians call the Old Testament.

theism—belief in a personal god (a being with mind, will, and emotions).

Theravada—Buddhist school closest to original teachings of the Buddha, mostly in Southeast Asia, that does not believe in celestial beings or a god.

Torah—Hebrew word for "teaching"; refers to both the Pentateuch (first five books of the Bible) and Jewish teaching in general.

ulama—Islamic scholars who reached consensus on what is true and right, based on their understanding of the *Qur'an* and *Hadith*.

Vedas—the Hindu scriptures, filling scores of volumes.

wu-wei—lit., "not doing"; the term in Daoism for going with the flow of the cosmic *Dao*.

yang—the active, warm, and light principle of the cosmos, according to Daoists.

yin—the still, cold, and dark principle of the cosmos, according to Daoists.

yoga—the way of meditation; refers both to a particular system developed by Pantanjali and to any systematic program of meditation.

Yom Kippur—Jewish Day of Atonement, in September or October.

Zen—school of Buddhism that emphasizes direct experience.

Zionism—the nineteenth-century, primarily secular Jewish movement to create a homeland, seeking respite from rampant anti-Semitism.

For Further Reading

Chapter 1 Hinduisms

Stephen Huyler. *Meeting God: Elements of Hindu Devotion.* New Haven, CT: Yale University Press, 1999.

R. C. Zaehner, ed. *The Bhagavad-Gita.* London: Oxford University Press, 1973.

Chapter 2 Judaism

Thomas Cahill. *The Gifts of the Jews: How a Tribe of Desert Nomads Changed the Way Everyone Thinks and Feels.* New York: Doubleday, 1998.

Milton Steinberg. *Basic Judaism.* San Diego: Harvest Books, 1975.

Chapter 3 Buddhism

Thomas Cleary, ed. and trans. *Dhammapada: The Sayings of the Buddha.* New York: Bantam, 1995.

Thomas Merton. *Zen and the Birds of Appetite.* Boston: Shambhala, 1993.

Donald W. Mitchell. *Buddhism: Introducing the Buddhist Experience.* New York: Oxford University Press, 1992.

Chapter 4 Confucianism and Daoism

Thomas Cleary, ed. and trans. *The Essential Tao.* San Francisco: HarperSanFrancisco, 1991.

Hans Küng and Julia Ching. *Christianity and Chinese Religions.* New York: Doubleday, 1989.

Thomas Merton. *The Way of Chuang Tzu.* Boston: Shambhala, 1992.

Chapter 5 Christianity

Philip Jenkins. *The New Faces of Christianity: Believing the Bible in the Global South.* London: Oxford University Press, 2006.

C. S. Lewis. *Mere Christianity.* San Francisco: HarperOne, 2001.

N. T. Wright. *Simply Christian.* San Francisco: HarperSanFrancisco, 2006.

Chapter 6 Shinto

Peter B. Clarke and Jeffrey Somers, eds. *Japanese New Religions in the West.* London: RoutledgeCurzon, 1994.

Sokyo Ono and William Woodward. *Shinto: The Kami Way.* North Clarendon, VT: Tuttle, 2004.

Chapter 7 Islam

Daniel Brown. *A New Introduction to Islam.* Malden, MA: Blackwell, 2004.

Thomas Cleary, ed. and trans. *The Essential Koran.* San Francisco: HarperSanFrancisco, 1993.

Mateen Elass. *Understanding the Koran: A Quick Christian Guide to the Muslim Holy Book.* Grand Rapids: Zondervan, 2004.